HERE COME THE RUSSIANS

The Diplomatic Visits to the United States by the Ministers Plenipotentiary (and Later Ambassadors) of the Russian Empire

S T E W A R T   L I L L A R D

Lulu Publishing Services rev. date: 09/25/2017

In memory of Prince
André Anatoliévitch Lobanov-Rostovsky
1892 - 1979

In honor of
Doctor Anastasia L. Koralova
Teaching Professor of Russian
University of North Carolina at Charlotte

LIST OF RUSSIAN MINISTERS
PLENIPOTENTIARIES AND AMBASSADORS, etc.

Count Fedor P. **Pahlen**
Andrei **Dashkov**
Nikolae Iakovievich **Kozlov**
Petr Ivanovich **Poletika**
Major General Diederik Jacob Van Tuyll Van Serooskerken
  (**Baron Van Tuyll**)
Baron de Maltitz
Pavel Alekseevich Krudener (**Baron Krudener**)
Baron d'Osten Sacken
Aleksandr Andreevich Bodisco (**Baron de Bodisco**)
Eduard Andreevich Stekl' (**Baron de Stoeckl**)
Constantine de Catacazy
Genrikh Genrikhovich Offenberg (Le Chevalier,
  Baron Henri d'Offenburg)
Nicholas **Shishkin**
Mikhail Fedorovich Bartolomei (**Michael Bartholomei**)
Kurill Vasil'evich Struv' (**Baron von Struve**)
Baron Roman Rosen
Prince Gregorii L'vovich Kantakuzen (**Prince Cantacuzene**)
Ernst Karlovich Kotsebu (Ernest **de Kotzebue**)
Mr. **de Wollant** [Vollant]
Artupr Pavlovich Kassini (**Count Cassini**)
Roman Romanovich Rozen (**Baron Roman Rosen**)
Georgii Yurii Petrovich Bakhmetev (**George Bakhmeteff**)
Boris Aleksandrovich Bakhmetev (**Boris Bakhmeteff**)

HERE COME
THE RUSSIANS

No, I am not referring to the American Cold War comedy film based on Nathaniel Benchley's novel, *The Off-Islanders*, which was directed by Norman Jewison and adapted for the screen by William Rose.[1] The diplomatic visits to the United States by the ministers plenipotentiary (and later ambassadors) from the Russian Empire throughout the 19th and early 20th century were far more historic than the fictitious Soviet submarine *Octopus* (Спрут), which ran aground on a sandbar off Cape Ann, Gloucester. These diplomatic visits were accompanied by Russian naval visits to the Atlantic and Pacific Coasts during the American Civil War, and several royal visits from members of the St. Petersburg court. What could be more exciting for an American audience than a glimpse of royal Russia on the very streets of Washington, D.C.?

During the mid 18th century, Russia kept watch on the British colonies in North America from a distance. Scientific correspondence was exchanged between Mikhail V. Lomonosov and Benjamin Franklin. The Russians even noticed the disturbances in Boston in response to the Stamp Act [March 22, 1765], the Boston Tea Party [December 16, 1773], the efforts of the American Continental Congress to cut off trade with Great Britain [1774], and the first armed clashes between British troops and American militia at Lexington and Concord on April 19, 1775. Russia and America,

1

however, were far apart geographically and politically. When asked by her fellow European monarch George III of the Great Britain, Empress Catherine II had to refuse to send Russian mercenaries to Canada to help Great Britain suppress the revolt in America (Catherine II to King George III, Sept 23 [Oct. 4 n.s.], 1775).[2] At first, Empress Catherine II had adopted limited liberal ideas, but by 1774 her own great empire had been in rebellion. Pugachev the Yaik Cossack had seized upon the peasants' unrest along the Volga River, and his rebellion had spread to most of the territories between the Volga and the Ural Mountains.[3] Not until General Michelsohn defeated the rebellious armies at Tsaritsyn [present Volgograd] at the end of 1774, and not until Pugachev was executed in Moscow's Red Square in January of 1775, did Catherine regain control of her own empire. The Americas had to wait.

Russia remained neutral during the American Revolutionary War and tried to "assist a reconciliation among the belligerent powers." When the Continental Congress (meeting in Philadelphia in December of 1780) sent Francis Dana to St. Petersburg, Russia, the Congress anticipated that Dana would "use every means which can be divised to obtain the concent and influence of that Court that these United States shall be . . . an independent nation." "You are to impress Her Imperial majesty . . . with a sense of justice of our cause."[4] John Quincy Adams, at fourteen years of age, dropped out of Harvard College to assist Dana as a secretary and translator for this 1781 trip.[5]

Dana "was unsuccessful in gaining recognition from the Russian Court and returned after fourteen months." Dana was never recognized by the Russian Court as a minister of state; and Her Imperial Majesty, Catherine II, returned a miniature portrait of George Washington (painted by Charles Willson Peale, 1777). The portrait had been sent to Francis Dana, who tried to present it to the Empress. Catherine rejected the miniature portrait and wrote that it is of someone Catherine "does not know"(1782). Russian officials were not to send or receive letters or packets from American intermediaries. After the American Revolutionary War in 1788, Empress Catherine

II received an American in the person of Naval Hero John Paul Jones. Jones "presented the Empress with a copy of the new American Constitution." "Her Majesty spoke to me often about the United States, and is persuaded that the American Revolution cannot fail to bring about others, and to influence every other government" (John Paul Jones to Marquis de Lafayette, June 1788). Yet, as late as 1795, Catherine was not recognizing an American Consul to her Court "out of friendship to Great Britain."[6]

Only after the death of Catherine II and Paul's ascendancy to the throne (1796) was the United States able to begin serious negotiations concerning "the establishment of mutual missions" between the two countries (1799). Furthermore, Paul I also saw the need for trade in furs with the Empire's North American territory and issued a royal decree [ukáse/указ] for the establishment of the Russian-American Company, July 8 [19 n.s.], 1799. (The U.S. and the Russian Empire were, throughout the next century, destined to become major Pacific Rim countries.)[7]

In October of 1803, Emperor Alexander I "deigned to recognize Levett Harris . . . in St. Petersburg in the capacity of Consul of the American States." This was the first significant diplomatic exchange between the two countries. Later that same year Emperor Alexander made it known that he would enjoy a correspondence with President Thomas Jefferson. In April of 1806, President Jefferson received a bust of Emperor Alexander. "The value of the bust derives from the great estimation in which its original [Alexander] is held by the world, and by none more than by myself," replied Jefferson.

Finally, in September of 1807, President Jefferson instructed James Monroe, envoy for the U.S. in Russia, to inform His Imperial Majesty of Jefferson's wish "to establish direct and immediate relations between Russian and the United States by appointing a Minister to reside there on his behalf." A year later in the summer of 1808, Emperor Alexander issued a decree establishing a Russian Consulate in the U.S. and appointing Andrei Iakovievich Dashkov as Consul General in Philadelphia (1809-1819). Aleksei G. Evstafev was simultaneously appointed Consul General to Boston.[8]

From the American side, William Short was appointed as Consular General to Russia by President Jefferson, but the U.S. Senate did not confirm this appointment as the members felt that the European situation with France and Napoleon did not warrant U.S. involvement on the continent. Jefferson left office on March 4, 1809. By summer, though, Count Fedor P. Pahlen had been appointed to the U.S. by Emperor Alexander as Minister (July 1810-July 1811); his contemporary Minister to Russia was John Quincy Adams, having been appointed by President James Madison and confirmed by the U.S. Senate. The diplomatic exchange from the American position was in full force. Except for a handful of American ministers, US appointees either did not take their posts seriously, or if they did manage the long arduous voyage, they stayed only one or two years. The Russian ministers who arrived in Philadelphia and then Washington found the climate and customs interesting and remained for far longer periods of assignments.[9]

When Andrei Dashkov arrived in Philadelphia in the summer of 1809, he described the "spirit of the Government" divided between two dominant groups: those who felt that the president was too weak "to give laws the necessary force and effect," and those who are "jealous of their liberty to excess . . . think they see attacks on their rights from all sides . . . and rebel against taxation in any form" (Dashkov to Rumiantsev, 1809). Dashkov then journeyed from his Chestnut Street residence in Philadelphia to Washington, D.C., to present his credentials to the Secretary of State and the President. He arrived one day and the next day was received by Secretary Robert Smith, who the following day, escorted the Russian minister to see President Madison. Dashkov dressed in full uniform as though he were going for an audience with the Emperor at the Winter Palace in St. Petersburg. In Washington, Robert Smith advised that "there was no particular protocol" but that a minister of a foreign government could have no contact with Congress except through the Secretary of State. After half an hour of conversation, Mr. Smith escorted me to the President's house. Between the State Department and the

Executive Mansion was "only a little garden" and we went by foot, wrote Dashkov.[10]

Dashkov may have been familiar with the formal stand-up presentation before a Russian Emperor as detailed in the Russian film *Russian Ark* [Русский Ковчег] directed by Alexander Sokurov (2002) when the Persian ambassador had to apologize for the death of a Russian diplomat, Alexander Griboedov, in 1829; but in the United States, President Madison "made me sit next to him."

> "When I remarked that it was time to take leave of the President, and stood up to make him my bow . . . he invited me to come dine at his home the next day. The President himself had only remained in the city to receive me."[11]

President Madison and his wife Dolley entertained Dashkov "as simple citizens." Dashkov was the General Counselor or Minister Plenipotentiary. He was supported in Washington by a counselor and secretary, Count Fedor P. Pahlen, who made a personal visit to Thomas Jefferson at his retirement home of Monticello, in Virginia, in May of 1811:

> "The country house where he lives is located in Virginia nearly 200 versts [212 kilometers] south of Washington.
>
> After having reached Monticello somehow or other by pretty bad roads, I found my stay there very rewarding. Mr. Jefferson joins the rare qualities of the statesman, the scholar, and the like-able man. His inquisitive mind covers all that is useful or interesting, his invention of a new plough speeds the progress of agriculture, and at the same time his astronomical observations rectify the geographical position of his country . . . He knows how to appreciate the rare qualities of a philanthropic Sovereign properly, and keeps his [Alexander I's] bust in his drawing room." (Fedor P. Pahlen to N. P. Rumiantsev, May 3 [15 n.s.], 1811)[12]

Count Pahlen was transferred to Brazil in November of 1811.

As 1812 began, Russia was still at peace with Napoleonic France and the United States was not at war with any European power. The month of June changed all that. Napoleon began his invasion of Russia which would culminate in the fall of Moscow on September 14th and the destruction of his *Grande Armee* throughout October and November. On June 18, 1812, furthermore, the U.S. declared war on the British Empire—a Second Revolutionary War! Through this initial period, the Russian minister, Andrei Dashkov, tried to negotiate between the U.S. and Great Britain. Russia wanted Britain to keep its troops in Europe and focused against Napoleon. The U.S., moreover, traded with Russian ports on the Baltic Sea; and war between the U.S. and Great Britain would halt this trade.[13]

Following the American victory at York (Toronto) in Upper Canada, April 1813, the Americans gained control of the Great Lakes and burned the British colonial capital. (A year later, the British army would return the favor by burning major governmental buildings in Washington, D.C.) With both the U.S. and Russia feeling a false sense of victory in their patriotic wars during the summer of 1813, political leaders in Virginia, Maryland and the District of Columbia proposed a large celebration to "hurrah" the Russian victory over Napoleon during Russia's First Great Patriotic War.

The political celebration and social event began in the Presbyterian Church of Georgetown (corner of Washington and Bridge [now M] Streets) on Saturday, June 5, 1813, beginning at 2 o'clock:

> "The ladies were first introduced into the church, then the members of the Senate and House of Representatives of the United States, members of the Maryland Legislature, strangers and Citizens of the District. One of the large pews in front of the pulpit was appropriated to the reception of the Presidents of the day [Thomas Sim Lee, Benj. Stoddert. Gen. Walter Smith, John C. Herbert, Daniel Carroll, Col. George Dencale, etc.] and the Consul of Spain. At half past two, the Russian Minister, his Lady, Counselor of Legation and Secretary, reached the church in his carriage of state."[14]

Old Presbyterian Church on the SE corner of Bridge and Washington Streets (now M and Washington Sts), Georgetown, DC. Scene of the political celebration in honor of Russia's victory over Napoleon, Saturday, June 5, 1813, beginning at 2 o'clock. Photograph from S[ally] Somervell Mackall, *Early Days of Washington* (Washington : The Neale Company, 1899), p. 109, & reprinted by G. E. Bishop Printing Co., Sterling, Illinois, 1934.

The Presbyterian minister, the Rev. Steven Balch, offered prayers, an oration was heard (possibly delivered by George Washington Parke Custis, Master of Arlington House[15]), and the parties were escorted to the Union Hotel across the street. At the end of the hotel's dining room was placed "an elegant portrait and a bust of the Emperor Alexander" supplied by Dashkov himself. Opposite the bust and portrait was placed a full-length portrait of Washington" painted in his youth and representing him "dressed in mililtary costume of the day." Then, "at 4 o'clock the company entered the dining rooms [of the Union Hotel] . . . a sumptuous entertainment had been provided . . . to which a company of upwards of two hundred and fifty gentlemen sat down." Over twenty toasts were offered (let's hope they were concluded with wine in place of Russian vodka). The Americans praised Field Marshall Konlonsoff, General Bagration, the Armies of Russia, the memory of George Washington, on and on. Mr. Swertchkoff, Counselor to the Russian Legation, toasted the fair sex of the United States: "May they never smile on the admirers of Bonaparte." Finally, Mr. Dashkov, the Russian Minister, toasted "prosperity to the United States . . . [may the U.S. be] no powerful enemy, no treacherous friend."

In a speech which may have been included in the Georgetown, D.C., ceremony, Robert Goodloe Harper, U.S. Senator from Maryland, condemned Napoleon at length:

> "That terror of his [Napoleon's] name, which appalled the hearts of his enemies and unnerved their arms, has been dissipated by the Russian sword . . . beaten, disgraced, compelled to repass [sic] the Russian frontier as a fugitive in disguise and to seek his own personal safety by the shameful abandonment of his followers in the hour of their danger and distress. Our hope . . . is in the final triumph of Russia. . . ."[16]

These citizens of the Mid-Atlantic states supported the Russian Empire in its first great patriotic war. The Russian leaders, in return, tried unsuccessfully to establish peace talks between Britain and the U.S. and to mediate the Anglo-American conflict. It is interesting to note, however, that no member of President Madison's executive branch of the national government was allowed to attend the Georgetown celebration "out of sympathy for France," the nation that had supported the U.S. in America's Revolutionary War.[17]

Dashkov, following the British burning of several government buildings in Washington City on August 24th, 1814, chose to reside in Philadelphia for several years. His reasons were that the District of Columbia could not supply "a reliable doctor" and he needed to "educate his . . . son."[18] In 1817, following the Kozlov affair, Minister Dashkov was recalled to Russia, but allowed to remain in Philadelphia until March of 1819. In this large city, Dashkov tried to fit-in with Philadelphia's upper class; but when he "displayed imperial symbols and crowns in the windows of his residence to mark the anniversary of Alexander I's coronation," a mob formed on the street and forced Dashkov to remove the symbols of monarchy. Shots were fired through his windows but no one was hurt.[19]

In November of 1815, Nikolae Iakovievich Kozlov, the Russian Consul in Philadelphia and a subordinate to Dashkov, was accused of raping a twelve-year-old servant in his home. The city authorities locked Kozlov in jail where he remained until the summer of 1816. Dashkov came to Kozlov's defense because a foreign diplomat had been arrested and subjected to local laws in violation of the "law of nations" which forbade local prosecutions. Charges were dropped in the city, but Kozlov was never convicted nor cleared of the charge of rape. Dashkov even "broke official diplomatic relation with the United States by the fall of 1816" over this incident. Finally, both Russia and the U.S. appointed new Chief Consuls and the Russians moved their primary residence from Philadelphia to the muddy streets of Washington City in the District of Columbia.[20] By 1820, the entire population of the District of Columbia was about 33,000, with 7,000 people residing in Georgetown, 8,000 in Alexandria, and

13,000 in Washington City. Farms filled portions of Washington County north of the Potomac River and Alexandria County south and west of the river.[21]

Petr Ivanovich Poletika served as an adviser to Count Pahlen in Washington (1809-11) and returned in 1819-22 as the minister plenipotentiary. While in the U.S. this second time, Poletika traveled widely and wrote *A Sketch of the Internal Conditions of the USA and of their Political Relations with Europe.*[22]

Poletika's replacement was Russian Army Major General Diederik Jacob Van Tuyll Van Serooskerken [Федор (Дидернк) Васильевич Тейль-Фан-Сероскеркен] who moved from a position of special minister to the King of Portugal in Rio de Janeiro to the Russian minister plenipotentiary to the U.S. from 1823-1826.[23] He rented the Decatur House on the west side of the President's Park [officially Lafayette Square after 1824] and made himself known as Baron de Tuyll. Before de Tuyll's arrival, the French Minister Baron Hyde de Neuville and his wife had rented the Decatur house.

Baron de Tuyll represented both the Russian Empire and the Holy Alliance (Russia, Austria, Prussia, etc.) while he was situated in the Americas.[24]

De Tuyll's use of the term "baron" dated from 1822 when the High Council of Nobility declared the Van Tuyll Van Serooskerken family as title *"noblesse immemoriale."* He, however, found that it was easier to be known in Washington as Baron de Tuyll. In a town of 13,247 free and enslaved inhabitants, Baron de Tuyll praised the village for its "venison, wild turkeys, canvas-backs [American ducks], oysters, terrapins," and gained a reputation as a "witty epicure" who lived alone and entertained often with excellent dinner parties. He thought Washington "furnished better viands [foods] than Paris, and only wants cooks."[25]

Before de Tuyll's arrival, the Russian-American Company had ventured south from Alaska in search of food supplies and sea otter pelts. Fort Ross, north of San Francisco Bay, was established by Ivan Kutskov in 1812 along the territory of Spanish California.[26]

Following the arrival of Baron de Tuyll in Washington City, the Baron was known as a "reactionary monarchist" who represented the Holy Alliance and who was pledged to restoring Europe's *ancient regime*, which meant restoring Spanish power to the recently freed South American countries.[27] His Russian Emperor, Alexander I, moreover, refused to receive or recognize any diplomat from the newly formed South American governments. "His Imperial Majesty . . . can not in any case receive near him any agent whatever, either of the administration of Colombia, or of any of the other Governments . . . which owe their existence to events, of which the new world has been for some years the theatre [revolution and freedom]" (Baron de Tuyll to Sec'y of State Henry Clay, Washington, Oct. 1823).

In 1821, Emperor Alexander issued a decree [ukáse/указ] declaring that all islands on the northwest coast of North America "extending from 51 degrees north (just above the northern point of Vancouver Island) had belonged to Russia from time immemorial."[28] Pierre de Poletica, Russia's Minister in Washington in 1821, staked Russia's claim "by right of first discovery." "The coasts of America as far down as 48 degrees north had been discovered and charted by Russian explorers."[29] Secretary of State John Quincy Adams (under President James Monroe) refuted the Russian claim and suggested that the Spanish discoverers had meant 58 degrees or 59 degrees north latitude. Both Great Britain and the U.S. objected to the claims in Alexander I's decree of 1821. British merchants, moreover, considered the decree a declaration of war against the commerce and fishing of British merchants to the north of the limits laid down by Russia.[30]

"Maison du Commodore Stephen Decatur, Washington, June 1822, by M[adame] E. [V]aile" Photograph used by permission of The White House Historical Association and The Decatur House, a National Trust Site. The Russian style of dress and coach would have been similar to the French style.

In the Atlantic Ocean sphere of influence, the defeat of Napoleon meant that reactionary powers had defeated liberal revolutions on the European continent. As Spain's former colonies in the American became independent, a vacuum existed in the Americas in which established European powers might replace the Spanish rule. The U.S. response was prepared by Secretary of State John Quincy Adams and included in President Monroe's State of the Union address presented to the Congress, on December 2, 1823. The famous document, although "thought-out" by Adams, became known as the Monroe Doctrine: the American continents were "no longer subject for future colonization by any European power," Any European political intervention in the Western Hemisphere would be "dangerous to our [U.S.] peace and safety"; on the other hand, "the U.S. would not intervene in European wars or internal concerns." This famous compromise, although introduced in U.S. school textbooks as a rejection of British, French, or Spanish interventions into the affairs of the newly liberated countries of Spain's former empire, became a block to Russia's penetrations along Mexico's California coast and down as far as Peru and Chile. The Monroe Doctrine was as important along the Pacific Coast as along the Atlantic Coast.[31]

Baron de Tuyll saw his Russian government forced to withdraw from its initial push along the Pacific Coast of the Americas.[32] In his mission, de Tuyll singularly failed. He was also thwarted at his rented home on Lafayette Square.

Following the duel on the west side of the Eastern Branch of the Potomac [Anacostia] River across from Bladensburg, Maryland, in which Stephen Decatur was killed on the morning of March 22, 1820, his widow, Susan Decatur, moved to a lesser address near Georgetown (Kalorama at the head of 21st Street) and rented her brick home on Lafayette Square, first to Baron and Baroness Hyde de Neuville, French Minister to the U.S. (1820-22) and then to Baron de Tuyll, the first Russian Minister to reside in Washington.[33] Over the four years that Baron de Tuyll rented the Decatur House, he was at times behind in his rent payments to the landlady.[34] De Tuyll also built a small "greenhouse" in the garden space without the permission of Susan Decatur. (St. Petersburg, Russia, was known for its "huge temples of shinning glass" where "all manners of fruits and vegetables were grown" . . . "in the art of forcing fruit and vegetables, Russian gardeners excel those of every other nation.")[35] Yet, to construct the green house, Susan Decatur was forced "to incur a most inconvenient disbursement in taking out a new and more expensive" policy of insurance. Then, when he was planning to return to Russia, de Tuyll ordered his servants "to tear down, sell and demolish" whatever the steward thought proper. Susan Decatur also accused the Russian minister and his steward of clipping her shrubbery and rooting it in the green house and selling the flowers and shrubbery from the grounds about the brick house. From her smaller home in Georgetown, the beautiful young widow was certainly on a course "to involve the two Nations in a long and bloody war" (Susan Wheeler Decatur to Sec'y of State Henry Clay, March 30, 1826).[36] To spite the steward's sale of the flowers and shrubbery from her rented home, Mrs. Decatur placed an unsigned notice in the town newspaper urging her friends "not to purchase from the domestics of the Baron de Tuyll" (*National Intelligencer*, March 23, 25, and 27, 1826).

A year earlier, Baron de Tuyll was known as a formal dinner host. Secretary of State John Quincy Adams wrote that he "dined with Baron Tuyll, the Russian Minister, it being the Emperor of Russia's birthday . . . the dinner . . . was, as usual on this occasion, diplomatic and formal."[37] Perhaps, the cabinet officer could visit de Tuyll's rented home on Lafayette Square. It was impossible for a U.S. president to visit a legation or embassy that belonged to a foreign government, a position to which Adams was elected and inaugurated in March of 1825.

Baron de Tuyll left Washington City in late March 1826 for a return to St. Petersburg due to his worsening physical condition, as he suffered greatly from gout. Many people believed he over indulged in alcohol and rich foods—"he preferred eating to socializing." He died on board the British packet *Francis Freeling*, on April 11, 1826, before the ship reached Halifax, Nova Scotia. His funeral took place in the harbor with military honors. He was 54 years of age at his death.[38]

On May 11th, a notice appeared in the Washington newspaper asking "all persons having claims against Anastase Anatagonni, Baron de Tuyll's steward" to present their accounts by May 13th.[39] A sale was also held which included "barouche, family carriage, horses, etc." "The carriage and horses are left at Mr. Robey's stable, on 8th st, where they may be inspected until the time of sale [P Mauro, auct.]."[40] [Some of the baron's furniture may have been sold to James Monroe and used in his retirement home in Virginia. Perhaps, also, Baron de Tuyll had sold off some furniture earlier in 1823 on his arrival to Washington, and this furniture was used by President Monroe in the White House.] [41]

On August 20th [Sept 1 n.s.], 1826, the acting minister of Russia, Baron de Maltitz, received a letter concerning a shipment of wine which arrived at the customs house in New York City and was addressed to the Russian Legation. Baron de Maltitz refused to pay for the Lisbon wine: "does not belong to it nor have any reason whatever to suppose that it ought to be consumed as part of the estate of the late Baron de Tuyll." Were the eight quarter casks of Lisbon wine ordered by the late Russian Minister in Washington and then refused by his subordinates after his death?[42] And, who benefited from drinking the Lisbon wine?

Finally, in June of 1833, following his second inauguration, President Andrew Jackson authorized the purchase of a "464-piece service of French Empire table silver" from the estate of the late Russian Minister de Tuyll. "Little of the flatware has survived . . . but almost all of the hollowware from the Paris shop of Martin-Guillaume Biennais (1764-1843)" remains in the White House collection today. The US National Archives preserves the bill of sale known as "Argenterie [Silver plate] . . . de M. le General Baron de Tuyll" and written about 1822 from Paris to Baron de Tuyll in Brazil where he was minister of Russia to the Portuguese King. The National Archives also preserves a note concerning the delivery of two leather and iron trunks to the President's House.[43] Baron Krudener was, in 1833, the Russian minister in Washington, having replaced Baron de Tuyll and Baron de Maltitz.

Recent Photograph of the entrance to the Stephen Decatur House, Lafayette Square, NW, Washington, DC. Photographed by Stewart Lillard.

Baron de Tuyll's recall to St. Petersburg and his unfortunate demise came at a crucial time in Russian history. Alexander I had died from food poisoning in Tagonrog on the Sea of Azov after returning from a tour of the villages of the Crimea, on the 19th of November 1825 (o.s.). Following de Tuyll's departure from Washington, Acting Minister Le Baron de Maltitz informed Secretary of State Henry Clay of Emperor Alexander's demise, on the 16th of May 1826, six months after the event. By the time the U.S. received formal news of Alexander's death, Russia had proclaimed Nicholas I (a younger brother to Alesander) as the new ruler and suffered a revolt by the Decembrists (Dec. 14, 1825, o.s.). One hundred and twenty men of this revolt were brought to trial, most of them exiled to Siberia, and several were hanged in July of 1826. Russia under Nicholas I and its new minister to the U.S., Baron Krudener, represented a total reset of diplomatic ties Paul Alekseevich Krudener [Павел Алексеевич Крюденер] represented the powerful autocrat Nicholas I from 1828-37 in Washington, arriving at the end of the John Quincy Adams administration and paralleling two terms of office of President Andrew Jackson.

To celebrate the inauguration of President Jackson, Baron Krudener (as he was known in Washington) gave a ball which was attended by the wife of General Porter [Letitia Breckinridge] and many others from the Adams administration. Krudener, like his predecessor de Tuyll, was a bachelor diplomat, but perhaps less formal and far more sociable with the ladies of the city. He resided on Pennsylvania Avenue near Georgetown.

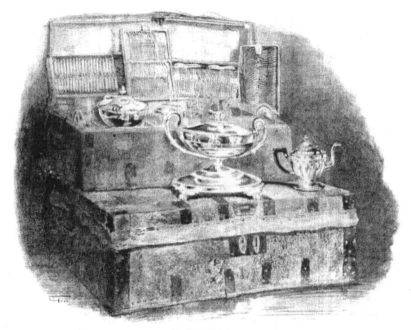

Drawn by Harry Fenn

THE BARON DE TUYLL CHESTS AND SILVER

The Baron de Tuyll Chest and Silver, from Abby G. Baker, "The White House Collection of Presidential Ware," *The Century Magazine*, vol. 76, n.s. vol. 54 (May to October, 1908), p. 833 [Drawn by Harry Fenn].

During Andrew Jackson's first term, his secretary of war, Major John Eaton, married the widow Peggy O'Neale Timberlake. Peggy and her father had owned the Franklin House tavern on I Street in D.C. The other cabinet wives simply would not mingle with Peggy and would not sit down at dinner parties with her even after Jackson and his Secretary of State Martin Van Buren arranged for both the British Minister Mr. Vaughn and the Russian Minister Baron Krudener to schedule diplomatic entertainments. Both Vaughn and Krudener were bachelors. [In death, both John and Peggy Eaton were buried near many prominent Washingtonians in Oak Hill Cemetery, Georgetown.] Reporter Henry Walker wrote years later that he remembered "Mrs. Peggy Eaton, the beautiful woman who was such a favorite of Old Hickory, and who practically caused the disruption of the Cabinet of the hero of New Orleans." [44]

Krudener, the Russian Minister, was excited about the proposed running of the first steam propelled railroad car from Baltimore to Ellicott's Mill, on the 28th of August, 1830. Early in 1830, Baron Krudener had ridden on a cart propelled by sails known as the *AEolus*. He sent a model of this wind experiment to his Emperor, Nicholas I. Now, he wanted to experience iron wheels on iron rails powered by a copper steam engine. (Russia's first train ran from St. Petersburg to Tsarskoye Selo in October 1837.) [45]

About this same time, Alexis de Tocqueville was visiting North America and compiling notes for his two volume work, *Democracy in America*, which first appeared in 1835. De Tocqueville wrote of "two great peoples on the earth . . . who, starting from different points, seem to advance toward the same goal . . . the Russians and the Anglo-Americans." "Each of them seem called by a secret design of Providence to hold the destinies of half the world in its hands one day." [46] Rail power was one means of judging that competitive progress. (The Russian empire would connect St. Petersburg with the Volga River at Nizhni-Novgorod by 1860 going eastward, and the U.S. would connect the Atlantic seaports with the Mississippi River going westward.)

During the Jackson administration, James Buchanan of

Pennsylvania was sent as an envoy to St. Petersburg. Buchanan left Washington in March of 1832 and arrived on June 2nd, in St. Petersburg. He had been prepared for court life under Nicholas I through talks earlier in Washington with Baron Krudener. Buchanan continued social contact with Krudener while the Russian minister was on furlough to St. Petersburg during the summer months of 1832.[47]

Baron Krudener's major diplomatic success was the negotiation of the first Commercial Treaty between the two countries which Nicholas I signed with the U.S. on December 18, 1832.

> "It was the first agreement of its kind which the Imperial Government had made with any nation, though others had long sought such a compact. It put the ships, cargoes, and crews of each country on a basis of reciprocity. The shippers of one country were to receive the same treatment in the ports of the other that they received in their home ports."[48]

Both Buchanan and Baron Krudener deserved much credit for this commercial treaty that remained in force for nearly a century. The main reason behind Russia's acceptance of the treaty, however, lay with its need for foreign friends. Russia had suppressed Polish independence in 1831 in the name of "orthodoxy, autocracy and national unity" and might need a major naval power that could import food and supplies to Baltic ports if Western European countries supported Poland.[49]

During the summer of 1832, with Baron Krudener in St. Petersburg, Baron D'Osten Sacken remained in Washington as an interim secretary. Sacken made objections to U.S. officials concerning articles that criticized Emperor Nicholas in the <u>Globe</u> newspaper, for the Russian Emperor was terribly sensitive to criticism . . . against him personally for instigating the horrible atrocities of the Polish War and for the enslavement of the Polish people."[50] President Jackson reasoned that if the American newspapers criticized the emperor over the Polish question, the same newspapers also criticized the American president far more over every item of Jackson's administration. Politicians in a democracy had learned to deal with such situations; autocratic emperors had not.

At the beginning of the administration of President Van Buren, the Russians sent Aleksandr Andreevich Bodisco [Александр Андреевич Бодиско] to Washington. De Bodisco had been born in Moscow on October 18, 1786 (o.s.). He had attended the Congress of Vienna in 1814 and was afterwards charge d'affairs at Stockholm. When he was posted to the U.S. in 1837, he was a middle-aged bachelor of 51 years and the eldest member of the diplomatic corps in the American capital.[51] The baron brought his two nephews, Waldemar and Borus Bordisco, with him and promptly enrolled them in Georgetown College where they graduated several years later with high honors. They probably were the best dressed and wealthiest members of the student body. The de Bodiscos were accompanied by the family steward Dona and by a handsome valet.[52]

In his first years as a diplomat in Washington, de Bodisco gave a Christmas party for his nephews Waldemar and Borus. The youth of Georgetown were invited, including the "beautiful Harriet Beall Williams, whom Mr. Bodisco saw there for the first time." He had other occasions to meet the 16 year old school girl in Georgetown, such as Miss English's school May party. It was love at first sight. The Williams family opposed the marriage at first, for de Bodisco seemed "too old and ugly." Miss Harriet had lost her mother and did not possess a large dowry. It was seen as a relationship of convenience with a large dose of love.[53]

De Bodisco and Harriet were married in June of 1840 at "four o'clock in the afternoon, at the Williams' home on Georgetown Heights." "Only the immediate relatives and the bridal party witnesses the ceremony, after which there was a brilliant reception." The bride was "given in marriage by Henry Clay." (President Martin Van Buren and Senator James Buchanan were part of the groomsmen.) The marriage and social events that followed took several days. One week later, Baron de Bodisco gave a grand ball and then President Van Buren "gave a handsome dinner at the White House in honor of Madame Bodisco" and another bride of the city.[54]

Baron de Bodisco and his young bride purchased an 1815 home in Georgetown known as the Clement Smith House. The home site was on south side 2 [2nd Street, now O St.], between Potomac and Frederick Streets [Frederick now named 34th St.], in the second block west of St. Johns Episcopal Church [Georgetown].[55] In 1845, Baron and Mrs. Bodisco were living in Cresswood, having purchased "a large tract of land called Argyle, Cowall and Lorn (about 300 acres between Rock Creek and Piney Branch)." The house stood at the corner of 18th and Varnum Streets [present Cresswood section, NW]. Following the Baron's death in 1854, the estate was sold to Thomas Blagden, a successful lumber merchant who operated a wharf on the Anacostia River west of the Navy Yard.[56]

The early 1840's saw an extension of U.S. influence in the Pacific Ocean, with a reduction of Russian, British and French influence. Several years before, Alexander I of Russia had tired to cut off the Bering Sea and preserve it as a Russian lake. Now, U.S. clipper ships were using the Sandwich [Hawaiian] Islands as a base for sailing to Alaska and the Bering Sea. Britain wanted ports in the Sandwich Islands to protect the Canadian coast and France also wanted ports in the same islands to protect the interests of Catholics in the Pacific area. Perhaps, between the social events, Baron de Bodisco was also looking out for Russian interests in the Pacific region.

Daniel Webster, Secretary of State, urged President John Tyler "to extend the Monroe Doctrine's opposition to European interference [in the Americas] to include Hawaii." Tyler's pronouncement of December 1842 became known as the Tyler Doctrine and established U.S. economic interests in the Sandwich Islands. Britain and France promised to respect the independent Kingdom of Hawaii.[57] During this same time, U.S. consuls had been sent to several cities in the Russian Empire: St. Petersburg, Riga [Latvia], Archangel, and Odessa [Ukraine].[58] To support Baron de Bodisco as Minister in Washington, several Russian consuls had been sent to the U.S., including Edward de Stoeckl, first secretary of the Legation in D.C.[59]

Baron de Bodisco's Home, also known as the Clement Smith House, 3322 "O" Street, Georgetown, NW, Washington, DC. The home was built in 1815, and from 1838 to 1854 this was the home of Alexander, Baron de Bodisco, Russian Minister to Washington. During the Civil War the house became a headquarters for Union officers. It was later divided and rented as apartments. Photo from S[ally] Somervell Mackall, *Early Days of Washington* (1899), p. 313, reprinted in 1934. See also: Robert Reed, *Old Washington, D.C., in Early Photographs, 1846-1932* (New York: Dover Publications, Inc., 1980), p. 157.

Senator and Mrs. John Kerry restored the former de Bodisco house on "O" Streeet, Georgetown. Photographed by Stewart Lillard.

Grave of Baron de Bodisco, located on Lot 3961/2 [Chapel Valley] in Oak Hill Cemetery, Georgetown, DC. Photographed by Stewart Lillard.

The 1840's decade was a period of U.S. and Mexican confrontation in the southwest. The U.S. acquired from the former Spanish Territory what was to be a quarter of the U.S. stateside land mass. But, that war and expansion was far from Washington City in the District. The Russian minister and his new bride, however, were often seen at lavish social events in the city. Secretary of State, James Buchanan, gave a ball in January of 1846, held at Carusi's Saloon, located at 11th and Pennsylvania Ave, NW, which was attended by more than a thousand guests. Two of the ruling social matrons present were Dolley Madison and Elizabeth Schuyler Hamilton. "Old Baron Bodisco's lovely teen-aged Georgetown wife wore a stunning set of diamonds that excited the envy of her sex." The guests dined on "venison, hams, beef, turkey, pheasant, chicken, oysters, lobster, ice cream, water ice, charlotte russe, punch, fruit and cake pyramids, blanc mange [sweet dessert], apple toddy, kisses, chocolate, coffee, 300 bottles of wine, 150 bottles of champagne, and harder beverages for harder drinkers."[60]

At another soiree at the country home in Kalorama [a classical home that stood where 23rd and S Streets, NW, presently are located], Dolley Madison described how "Count Bodisco holds a private levee at one end of the room, and all the world is introduced." "The French, British and other Ambassadors cluster together, glittering in uniforms and the crosses of foreign orders and frightful moustaches and beards." In such a crowd, the short [President] James Knox Polk, was "forgotten." In her seventies, Dolley Madison found the affected manners of the foreign diplomatic corps absurd, the band's playing was too loud, and the "chatting, laughing, and coquetting" difficult to endure after the president had made his brief remarks.[61] Perhaps, these social events were a wonderful way for the Baron de Bodisco to gain bits of information from his rival ministers, but the elderly ladies preferred not to talk of business.

The Russian Minister, Alexander de Bodisco, died at his Georgetown residence on O Street, NW, on the 23rd of January 1854, just as Russia was about to go to war with Britain and France. He was buried in Oak Hill Cemetery, just east of the Corcoran

Chapel. Widow Harriet Williams Bodisco went on an extended tour; in India she met a British army officer, Captain Douglas Gordon Scott. On May 29th, 1860, Widow Bodisco married Capt. Scott at St. John's Episcopal Church on Lafayette Square, across from the White House. The Rev. William Norwood, rector of Christ Church, in Georgetown (the home church of the Bodiscos and the Williams) presided over the noon wedding and President James Buchanan gave away Mrs. Bodisco.[62]

The late Baron de Bodisco had left his family an estate of almost $300,000 US dollars.[63] He owned $40,000 US dollars worth of various US railroad bonds.[64] Concerning the two nephews whom Baron de Bodisco had brought with him from Russia and educated at Georgetown College, it is noted that Waldemar returned to Russia and married Annette Bodisco, his cousin whom he later brought to Georgetown. Waldemar was, in 1878, the Russian consul general in New York City. He suffered from "congestion of the lungs." He went to the Jordan Alum Springs, Virginia, for a cure, but died in July of 1878. Waldemar was buried in Oak Hill Cemetery along with his uncle. His wife and three sons survived him and remained in New York City. At Waldemar's funeral, the body-bearers included Admiral Semetchkine, aid-de-camp to the Grand Duke Constantine, and Brooke B. Williams, father of Harriet Bodisco of Georgetown.[65] Borus, the other nephew, returned to Russia, chose a military career, married and remained in his native country.

The children of Baron Alexander and Harriet Bodisco scattered. Alexander died abroad and his remains were buried in Oak Hill Cemetery. William went to Russia and was working in government service. Costa Bodisco married the daughter of Joseph Barton of Georgetown, Charlotte Barton. In 1878, they lived in Russia. When he died in 1896, Costa [Constantine] and Charlotte Barton Bodisco had a daughter, Olga Bodisco, who had been invited to be a maid of honor for the coronation of Nicholas II, but she had to decline. Baron de Bodisco also had two daughters: Olga married abroad, and Mittie Bodisco chose to move to England and live with her mother.[66]

It is also interesting to note that when nephew Waldemar de

Bodisco died in Virginia in July of 1878, three businesses placed claims against his estate: Georgetown College, a tailor of Baltimore, and his dentist. The estate owed the most to Georgetown College for the education of his three sons, Alexander, Boris, and Waldemar. On the reverse of the college bill two words in Russian Cyrillic were written in bold ink, perhaps written by Annette de Bodisco, his widow, who was born and educated in Russia. Written on the probate document are the only Cyrillic words in the existing legal papers: Католическая Школа [Catholic school], $582.00.[67]

Eduard Andreevich Stekl' [Эдуард Андреевич Стекль] became Envoy Extraordinary and Minister Plenipotentiary to the U.S. in 1854 and remained in that position for fifteen years of heightened activities between the two rising empires. When the middle-aged diplomat left St. Petersburg in the winter of 1853, he thought he was to be a consul-general to the Sandwich [Hawaiian] Islands. He landed in New York and learned of the death of Baron de Bodisco and that he was expected to take charge of the U.S. assignment where he had spent some years as de Bodisco's assistant. Baron de Stekl' took up residence at the corner of Connecticut and "I" Streets, NW. Other members of the Russian legation resided on "K" Street, between 16th and 17th Streets, NW.[68]

The events of the 1850's and 1860's forced Russia and the U.S. into each other's embrace. In 1848, Europe felt the quakes of revolutions and freedom fighters on barricades. Hungary, led by Louis Kossuth, won a brief independence from the Austrian Empire. The armies of Emperor Nicholas I of Russia then crushed the Hungarian revolution. When Kossuth toured the U.S. on behalf of the Hungarian revolt, Abraham Lincoln gave Kossuth his support in 1852. In fact, Lincoln spoke in favor of freedom fighters in Hungary, Ireland and the German States. During the same time, Russia was considered "the stronghold of reaction and the most hated and despised nation in Europe."[69]

The U.S. should have supported Great Britain against Napoleonic France in 1812 and she should have supported Great Britain during the Crimean War (1853-6) against Russia; but the lingering hatred of Great Britain originating from the time of the Revolution and the fight for independence caused the U.S. to join with opponents of Britain. In the spring of 1855, Jefferson Davis, Secretary of War to President Franklin Pierce, sent "three American army officers to Russia . . . to study and . . . observe the war in Crimea." (Incidently, three hundred riflemen from Kentucky volunteered to fight in Sevastopol in the service of the tsar.) Russia had proposed to act "as mediator in the War of 1812" between Britain and the U.S. Now, the U.S. proposed to act as a mediator in the Crimean conflict between Russia and Western European powers.[70] (During the U.S. Civil War, Russia would again offer to mediate between the Federal and Confederate governments, but the Lincoln administration would not allow such peace efforts to proceed.)[71]

Baron de Stekl' had been born in Istanbul in 1804. He was the son of an Austrian diplomat in Istanbul and a maternal grandson of Nicolas Pisani, a Russian in Istanbul.[72] In Washington, in 1856, Eduard de Stekl' married Elizabeth Howard, "an American Protestant without property. . . ." Elizabeth was "stately as a queen and beautiful"; Eduard was "tall and aristocratic" with a face covered with "side whiskers and a mustache." Elizabeth was a "cleaver woman who helped her diplomat husband win his way into the best society in Washington." Eduard had friends on Capitol Hill, "wining and dining in their company and frequently relaxing with them over gambling tables" of the city. De Stekl' was friends with several presidents: he was a guest at the White House, conferred with secretaries of state (especially William H. Seward of Lafayette Square) and other members of the cabinet, kept contacts with army officers, newspaper correspondents, and other sources of information.[73]

As early as the 1840's, Emperor Nicholas I had been willing to sell off Russian America [Alaska, Аляски]. The fur trade had run its course, only about a thousand Russians still lived in Alaska, and the empire had an insufficient navy in the Pacific Ocean to supply the coast of Alaska with fresh fruit and vegetables. From a political point, in case of hostilities in Europe over the Polish situation or the Black Sea region of the Crimea, the Russian Empire could not defend its

North American Company from either British or American attacks from the sea. When Nicholas I appointed Count Nikolai Muravyev Amurskiy as Governor General of Siberia in 1847, the Emperor chose a visionary who proposed a strong Russian presence on the western shores of the Pacific Ocean and a friendly U.S. presence on the eastern shore. Russia should look to turning over her American territories to the U.S. Under Gov. Muravyev's able administration, the Russian Empire occupied the mouth of the Amur River, established Nikolayevsk-on-Amur as a naval port in 1856 and occupied Sakhalin Island. There was no Pacific fleet to defend or supply Russian Fort Ross in California (1812-1841), a proposed fort in the Sandwich Islands, nor the Alaskan settlements. Muravyev-Amurskiy solidified Russian claims along the Amur River on the continent and cut lose the overseas colonial attempts made by Russia.[74]

Baron de Stekl's first official duties as Minister Plenipotentiary in Washington included a formal appearance at President James Buchanan's inauguration and ball on March 4, 1857. The ball was held in a wooden pavilion constructed near the District of Columbia courthouse in Judiciary Square. (Buchanan had served as an envoy to St. Petersburg during the administration of Andrew Jackson and had once attended a Te Deum service in the company of Emperor Nicholas I at the Alexander Nevsky Lavra.) "While dancing at the inauguration ball with Madame de Sartiges, wife of the French Minister, [De Stekl', during the dance] commented that the current crisis in Washington [over slavery] compared with the situation in Paris just before the revolution of 1830" when Talleyrand whispered to Emperor Louis Philippe at the Palais Royal, "We are dancing on a volcano."[75]

To insure he kept his superior, Prince Alexander Mikhailovich Gortchakov, Minister for Foreign Affairs, fully informed of the turmoil in the American government, Baron de Stehl' wrote at length of James Buchanan as possessing "a glaring lack of the qualities necessary for a Chief Executive of a great nation." "The failures of Mr. Buchanan are due to the weakness of his character aggravated by his advanced age" and "excessive egotism." In addition, de Stehl' described Lincoln as a man of "agreeable and honest expression," a man of "manners . . . who spent all his life in a small Western town," "polite and engaging" but "weak, undecided, inexperienced." On the other hand, de Stekl' described "Mr. Jefferson Davis . . . [as] one of the most remarkable men in the United States." He was one of the "cold and energetic characters who never draw back from any obstacle." Both de Stekl' and Gortchakov "feared for the breakup of [Russia's] only diplomatic friend." "Politically America will cease to be a great nation" if the sections separate and lose their political importance.[76]

Much has been written about the *entente cordial* that existed between President Lincoln and Emperor Alexander II, in the 1860's. Perhaps, it is easy to explain how two very different countries could develop a friendship from afar. Internally, Alexander II had, one day before Lincoln's inauguration (March 3, 1861 / Feb. 19 o.s.), signed the Emancipation Reform that freed millions of Russian serfs over a two-year period. President Lincoln's Emancipation Proclamation took effect on January 1, 1863, and freed the slaves in Confederate territories that were still in rebellion. Europe, moreover, was experiencing a rise of independence in the Polish-Lithuanian Commonwealth, which by 1863 became an uprising against the Russian Empire.[77] Of interest on the diplomatic side, Russia and the U.S. agreed in 1861 "to cooperate to establish a telegraph cable connection between St. Petersburg and San Francisco by way of the Bering Sea and Siberia"—a formidable task left undone because of distance and terrain.[78]

During the American Civil War, Russia was able to use its diplomatic friendship with the Americans in a secret effort to relocate its naval vessels to warm-water friendly ports at a time when Russia was opposing French and British efforts in support of Polish independence.[79] In reality, the wooden Russian naval vessels were of little use to the US forces and diplomatically had to be kept out of harm's way. "From the safe American coasts the Russians would be in a favorable position for cruising against British commerce in the Atlantic and the Pacific, should war suddenly break out over the tempestuous Polish question."[80] By June of 1863, Russia expected Britain and France to declare war in Europe in defence of Polish freedom.

The Russian navy formed two cruiser squadrons and sent them to anchor in US ports. At the suggestion of the American Secretary of the Navy, Gideon Welles, the Baltic Squadron under Rear Admiral Stepan Lesovskii would sail to the Brooklyn Navy Yard, NY, and the Pacific Squadron under Rear Admiral Andrei Alexandrovich Popov would sail to Mare Island Navy Yard across from San Francisco, California.[81]

The two Russian squadrons arrived at their destinations by late September of 1863 and remained until the August 1864 departures. The Baltic squadron contained the *Osliaba, Variag, Vitiaz, Peresvet,* and the *Alexander Nevsky.* [In Russian history, two monks, Alexander Peresvet and Osliaba had accompanied Dmitri Donskoi (1363-1389) against the Tatars at the Battle of Koulikovo Field (1380). The *Vitiaz* (1861-1900) was named for a South Sea straight.] Several clippers also arrived. Mrs. President Lincoln also arrived in New York City during this same week and "created a great *furore.*"[82]

When the tall-masted Russian ships, "flying red, white and blue Imperial flags" dropped anchor in New York Harbor, one of their young officers on board was Rimskii-Korsakov. He stayed in the United States from September 1863 until August 1864. Rimsky "visited Annapolis and Baltimore and went up the Hudson to Albany and then to Niagara Falls." In New York City, Rimsky "visited restaurants and lounged about eating and occasionally drinking" and also "heard a poor performance of Gounod's *Faust.*" Soon after the squadron anchored in New York Harbor, a grand ball was held at the Academy of Music, "where hoop-skirted ladies were whirled about by Russian and Union officers."[83] Admiral Lisovskii reportedly "protested such frivolity and extravagance during war time."[84] This banquet and ball was scheduled for mid-October, as "at least ten days will be required to prepare the table ornaments and other decorations suitable to the occasion"[85] Following the events of October, the newspaper reported that "more accomplished, gentlemanly, and prepossessing guests than the Russian officers have never visited the City."[86]

Rear Admiral S. S. Lisovski and His Officers, photographed by
Mathew Brady, ca. 1863-4. (Pictured left to right): Captain Lieutenant
P. A. Zelenoi (*Almaz*); Captain First Rank I. I. Bytakov (*Osliaba*);
Captain Fedorovsky (*Alexander Nevsky*); Rear Admiral Lisovski;
Grand Duke Konstantin Nicholaevish (Admiral of the Imperial Navy
and brother of Emperor Alexander II, who accompanied the fleet on
its historic visit); Captain Lieutenant P. V. Kopitov (*Peresviet*); and
Captain Lieutenant R. A. Lund (*Variag*). Naval History & Heritage
Command, Washington, DC. Image number: NH 47604.

"Group of Russian Sailors from the navy ship Variag' [Варягъ] during the visit to New York City." Library of Congress, LC-DIG-cwpb-05384 [reproduction number]. The four men at center are boatswain's mates, as indicated by the call (whistle) worn as part of their uniform.

The autumn season in New York was a wonderful time for the officers and members of the crews to enjoy themselves "in their own way in viewing the sights of the City, and partaking individually of the hospitalities" of the Americans. One evening, Admiral Lisovskii "visited Niblo's Theatre to witness Mlle. Vestvali's personation of the Jewish Mother."[87] [Felicita Vestvali of Krakow performed *Gamee*, or the Jewish Mother, at Niblo's Garden at the corner of Lower Broadway and Prince Street.]

This naval visit also illustrated a great distance between American and Russian cultures. The newspaper correspondent wrote at length of the "most interesting novelties of the Russian fleet . . . the Chaplain—a Greek priest." The Greek [Orthodox ?] priest is "dressed in the fashion of South American *padres*, except that the hat, instead of being low-crowned, with an immense wide-leaf, is a good deal of the 'stove pipe' fashion:

> There is one of these clergymen on all vessels of any magnitude, and two on very large ones. On Sunday mass is celebrated on the open deck, after the manner of the Greek Church, the language used during the celebration of the ceremony being Greek [Church Slovanic ?] The *padre*, of course, has a wife and family, and, like the wives of all other officers, they have to remain on shore while their husbands are at sea. A superficial observer visiting the gundeck of the flagship, would think that he was entering a Spanish or French vessel. An attempt to illustrate the different passages in the Scriptures in a pictorial way is made, the spaces between the guns being decorated with images of saints and of the blessed Virgin, in various stages, and likenesses of almost every saint in the calendar. Of course, to a person not versed in saintly theology, these *figures* are very mystical, indeed. The *padre* . . . wears a full beard, which falls upon his breast, and rather long, dark, curling hair. His large

blue eyes are full; his form is well filled out, and all his movements are dignified and noble. He is as intelligent as he is amiable.[88]

Soon after these social events in New York, invitations from other East Coast cities reached the Russian fleet. Boston, Baltimore, and Washington all wanted the exotic fleet to visit their naval yards.[89]

The late summer season of August 1863 was also a perfect time for Secretary of State Seward to lead a two-weeks tour of upstate New York with foreign ministers "including those of England, France, Spain, Germany, and Russia." "Seward had engineered the trip to counter the impression abroad that the lengthy war was starting to exhaust the resources of the North." The group "journeyed up the Hudson, stopping in Albany, Schenectady, and Cooperstown," in anticipation of the fall entertainment which would be offered to the Russian naval officers and crew. The diplomats "sailed the Finger Lakes, visited Niagara Falls, and spent the night in Auburn [Seward's home], where they were joined by Seward's neighbors and friends for a picnic on the lake."[90] A photo from this trip shows Baron Edward de Stoeckel [Stekl'] the Russian Minister seated at the foot of an unidentified waterfall [Trenton Falls ?] with Seward and Count Waldemar de Bodisco, the nephew of the former Russian minister to the US.[91]

Diplomats at the foot of an unidentified waterfall [Trenton Falls ?],
New York State, August 1863. Secretary of State, William H. Seward
is seated with hat in hand near the right; Count Waldemer de Bodisco,
nephew of the former Russian Minister to the US, third from left
with tall white hat; and Baron Edward de Stoeckel, Russian Minister,
is seated second from right, with a tall black hat. National Archives
Identifier: 518056, selected list identifier #29, NAIL Control number,
NWDNS-59-DA-43.

Baron de Stoeckl, part of the Brady-Handy Photograph Collection. Library of Congress. LC-USZ62-128254 [reproduction number]. LC-DIG-cwpbh-02874 [reproduction number].

In November of 1863, the Russian squadron stationed in New York Harbor sailed down to Hampton Roads, Va., and up the Potomac River and docked at the north end of the Alexandria wharf. Congressmen, members of the Cabinet, and distinguished citizens were entertained at a banquet aboard the *Osliaba*, and later the President and Mrs. Lincoln gave a brief reception at the White House.[92] Even today, Colgate University's Case Library contains Civil War photographs that include one photo of "crew members of an unidentified warship of the Imperial navy that visited the U.S.," probably taken at Alexandria, Virginia, in 1863.[93] Other libraries also contain copies.

On the 18th of December 1863, President Lincoln was "greeted with loud applause at Willard's Hotel in Washington, DC, as he arrived for a lecture on Russia by the diplomat Bayard Taylor." Also, during the December holidays of 1863, Secretary of State William H. Seward who lived on the east side of Lafayette Square in front of the President's Mansion, "entertained the members of the visiting Russian fleet [officers only ?] in his usual lavish style: a four-course meal, served with an unlimited supply of the best wine." "As the ladies took tea in the parlor, the men adjourned to the sitting room, where . . . the conversation would often be continued for two or three hours in a cloud of smoke."[94]

A week before the Potomac River "iced up," the Russians sailed down the river for winter ports: one ship remained at Hampton Roads, Va., three ships went to unknown ports in the West Indies, and two ships harbored at Annapolis on the larger Chesapeake Bay.[95]

Admiral Popov and his Pacific squadron were entertained equally well in San Francisco and the visit remained the high point of the city's social life from September 1863 through August of 1864. The Russians assisted the city following a fire on the night of October 23, 1863; and another time the officers were feted at a ball where Admiral Popov lost his hat.[96]

Crew of the Russian frigate *Osliaba* [*Осляба*] docked north of the main pier at Alexandria, Va., 1863. National Archives Indentifier: 518113, selected list identifier # 31, NAIL Control number, NWDNS-64-CV-210. Also, Library of Congress Prints and Photographs Division, Washington, DC. Photographer, Andrew J. Russell. LC Bookmark: http://www. loc.gov/pictures/item/2006681145/

The question might arise as to why the port of San Francisco needed protection from hostile Confederate (CSA) ships so far away from the land war and on the Pacific Ocean. CSA naval records do, however, record mention of the CSA naval pirate, Rafael Semmes (1809-1877) who captained the *CSS Alabama*, around Capetown, South Africa, and in the Pacific Ocean. The *CSS Shenandoah* ended its naval operations in the Bering Sea after having taken eleven whalers as prisoners on June 2, 1865. The *CSS Shenandoah* surrendered to the British at Liverpool, England, in November of 1865. San Francisco, far from the US naval "Anaconda" blockade in the Atlantic Ocean, felt protection behind the Russian ships from several potential raiders. The goodwill that developed from the Russian's Pacific and Atlantic fleets "lasted for many years."

Whether of not the enlisted seamen or young officers had contact with the many women of the night who had flocked to Washington to be near the American troops and who were called "hooker's women" after General Hooker the commander of the Washington Military District, no record of this liaison remains.

One encounter between a Russian seaman and members of an American shore party does remain recorded in the Annapolis National Cemetery, Section G, Grave # 2420 that of N[ikolai] Demidoff, who was killed in Annapolis, MD., on February 4, 1864. Demidoff had been assigned to the flagship *Almaz* [*Almay*], the same ship on which the eighteen year-old recent graduate of the Russian naval academy, Rimskii-Korsakov, sailed. While the ship waited for warmer weather to return to Russia and Northern Europe, the sailors on this good will tour "wandered through Annapolis' streets." As the Russian sailors were visiting several of the town's saloons around the wharf, "one barkeep refused to serve the [Russian] group as they were already fairly inebriated; Demidoff took offence and began to hassle the barkeep." US cavalrymen in the same saloon helped the barkeep remove the drunken foreign sailors from the premise. Outside, the drunken seamen "assailed their escort and fled." "Pursued by the cavalrymen the Russians fled" into a hotel owned by William T.

League, where "in the course of an argument" Demidoff was shot by William League. Demidoff was shot on Thursday night and buried on Saturday "after the manner of the Greek [Russian ?] Church" as reported in the *Baltimore American* newspaper. The funeral service began in the chapel of the Naval School [Academy] which was crowded.[97]

> The remains of the deceased were laid out in a neat walnut coffin in the center of the chapel, accompanied by the officers and sailors of the two Russian vessels in port. A full Orthodox liturgy for the burial of the dead followed, led by a priest from the Russian ships. Following the service the remains were conveyed in mournful procession from the Chapel to the open space in front of it and then through the city . . . to the military burial ground about one mile from Annapolis, where the last rites of the church were performed. Dr. Vanderkeift, the Surgeon in charge of the Naval School, was unremitting in his attentions to the Russian visitors and superintended all the arrangements for the funeral.[98]

The Russian Minister to the U.S., Baron de Stekl', attended the burial service for Sailor N. Demidoff and walked through the streets of Annapolis in the funeral parade from the Navel School to the military cemetery on the west side of the town.

The people of Annapolis and the State of Maryland were so upset by the death of Demidoff that the House of Delegates of the General Assembly, meeting on February 5, 1864, the day after the shooting, passed a resolution by 54 affirmative to 8 negative votes as follows: "Whereas, One of the crew of the Russian ships, now in the harbor of Annapolis, was killed by a citizen yesterday . . . And, Whereas, We consider them the guests of the Nation, it therefore becomes our duty to them as strangers, in a strange land, not understanding our language or customs, to do something to vindicate ourselves from the appearance of inhospitality. . . ." Five days later, the Delegates unanimously voted: "Whereas, There happily exists between the Russian nation and our own the liveliest feelings of friendship, and a high regard for the exalted greatness and grandeur of each other . . . a committee of seven . . . is hereby created, with instructions to visit the Russian naval vessels now in the Severn river, and extend to the officers . . . a cordial invitation to visit . . . consistent with their pleasure and convenience."[99]

Across the bay from San Francisco, California, six Russian sailors were buried in the Mare Island Cemetery. On the night of October 23, 1863, a fire broke out in San Francisco. Russian Rear-Admiral Popov dispatched 200 officers and sailors from the corvette *Bogatyr'* to the landing at the Embarcadero [Eastern waterfront and piers]. Three of the Russian sailors were injured during the fire, but none of the ships' logs recorded a death from the fire. Popov logged the deaths of Artemy Trapeznikov, sailor, deceased, Oct 27, 1863, died of typhoid fever; a Russian sailor, deceased, Nov. 20, 1863, possibly musician Kort, but no cause of death; and Iakov Butorin, sailor, deceased, Dec. 29, 1863, with no cause of death in the log. Russian ships *Abrek* and *Novik* also reported deaths from individuals found in sick bay, or due to consumption, or one drowning from a mishap at sea.[100]

The Russian squadrons returned to European and Pacific waters in 1864. Emperor Alexander II, in August, expressed to Casius Clay [US minister to Russia], at Peterhof Palace [outside St. Petersburg], "the profound gratitude of the Emperor of All the Russians for the help and cooperation granted to his navy and the favors and kindnesses bestowed upon the officers and crews."[101]

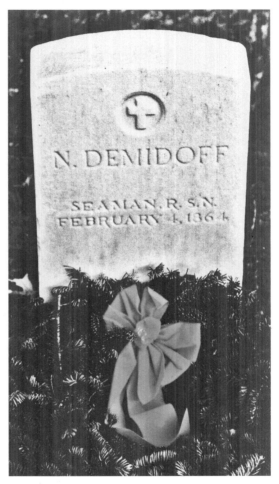

Grave Stone of Nikolai Demidoff, Military Cemetery, Annapolis, Maryland. Photographed by Stewart Lillard.

Russian Pacific Fleet, Mare Island, California, 1864. Lithograph. Naval History & Heritage Command, Washington, DC. Image Number: NH.91516. (l. to r.) *Rynda, Bogatyr',* and *Kalevala.* [Not pictured, *Novik, Abrek,* and *Gaidamak.*]

Stateside, Russian Minister Baron de Stekl' was busy: he conferred with President Lincoln, offered suggestions to American generals, asked the Secretary of War about troop strengths, obtained plans of battles, sought the "designs and blueprints of the ironclad *Monitor* and even sent them to St. Petersburg. (Russia had built a thin coated metal ship in 1861 that was not well suited for rough ocean travel.) De Stekl' even regreted that no Russian naval officer had been present to observe and record the battle between the *USS Monitor* and the *CSA Virginia* [*Merrimac*] in March 9th of 1862 off Hampton Roads,Va.[102]

Baron de Stekl's most significant duties in Washington during 1864 and 1865 consisted of attending Lincoln's second inaugural ceremony in March and then helping President Andrew Johnson review the Union troops in late May of 1865, the Russian minister "in full court costume," in the victory parade along Pennsylvania Avenue.[103] He, too, arranged for the sending of a U.S. special envoy in a naval vessel to Russia "to convey in person to His Imperial Majesty America's good will and congratulations 'to the twenty million of serfs upon providential escape from danger of the Sovereign to whose head and heart they owe their freedom.'"[104] Lincoln had been assassinated in Washington on April 14, 1865, and died the following day. Emperor Alexander II had escaped an assassination attempt in St. Petersburg, at the hands of Dmitri Karakozov, on April 4, 1866. The naval mission to Russian was led by the Hon. Gustavus Vasa Fox, Assistant Secretary of the U.S. Navy. In addition, the U.S. sent an ironclad monitor, *Miantonomoh*, to the Russian naval base at Kronstadt off St. Petersburg. Accompanying the *Miantonomoh* were the two wooden men-of-war, *Augusta* and *Ashuelot*. This good will voyage lasted from June through August of 1866; and Rear Admisal Lisovski received the Americans, even taking them to the Trade Fair in Nizhnii Novgorod on the Volga River east of Moscow.[105]

Gustave Vasa Fox, carte de visite, photographed by [Rafail] Livitsky, or his father, Lergey Lvivich Levitsky, No. 30 Moika Canal, Saint Petersburg, Russia. Library of Congress Prints and Photographs Division, Washington, DC. LC Bookmark: http://www.loc.gov/pictures/item/2005677225/

Prior to the voyage to St. Petersburg, Commodore Craven of the U.S. Navy, commanding the *USS Niagara* in port at Lisbon, Portugal, sought permission to accompany Admiral Lisovski and the *Alexander Nevsky*, the *Oleg* and yacht *Almaz*, from Lisbon to Kronstadt, Russia, bearing the remains of the late Grand Duke of Russia who had died while traveling in Europe. Nicholas Alexandrovich, eldest son of Emperor Alexander II, and heir to the throne, made a tour of southern Europe in early 1865 where he contracted an ailment [spinal-meningitis]. He died in Nice, France, on April 24, 1865 (ns). His remains were being returned to Russia by Admiral Lisovski. Such were the friendly relations between the Russian and U.S. navies in the 1860's.[106]

Earlier in the 1850's, President James Buchanan had inquired about the possibilities of an American purchase of Russian North America [Alaska] to prevent the British from further expansion along the Pacific Coast. The American purchase money would have helped Russia pay its expenses incurred during the Crimean War of 1853-56. By the mid 1860's, some critics of the proposed purchase of Alaska debated whether the U.S. should give the Russian Empire the $7,200,000 dollars in return for Russia's diplomatic aid during the American Civil War and let Russia keep the "frozen, barren wasteland" of Alaska.[107]

A short time following the successful naval visit of Gustavus Vasa Fox to Russia, negotiations for the purchase of Alaska were concluded. This era of good will between the two countries and the similarities of personal tragedies between President Lincoln's family and Emperor Alexander's family may have encouraged members of Congress to approve the purchase. Russia sold nearly 600,000 sq. miles of territory to the USA for $7.2 million in gold. The U.S. took possession of Alaska on October 18, 1867, at Sitka, when the Russian flag was exchanged for the Stars and Stripes. Congress did not approve the funds for the sale until July 14, 1868, in a special session of Congress;[108] and warrants for the purchase were placed in the Riggs Bank in Washington (August 1, 1868) and then sent to New York for ship passage of the gold bullion [coins]: "Pay to

Edouard de Stoeckl, Envoy Extraordinary . . . Seven Million Two Hundred Thousand Dollars," Treasurer, U.S., F. E. Spinner."[109] [Dft. No. 9759 on Treasury Warrant No. 927, ARC Identifier 301667, U.S. National Archives, Washington, DC] The proclamation of the sale of Alaska was published as Bozhiey posp'shestvuyshchey milostiy my Aleksandr' Vtoryi . . . and signed *Ob'yavlyaem' chrez'* [By means of the declaration].[110] Baron de Stekl' signed a receipt at the U.S. Treasury Department in Washington for the total sum in "coins being the full amount due from the United States to Russia" agreed to in the treaty of March 30, 1867.[111] [U.S. National Archives, ARC Identifier 301666, Draft for Payment for the Purchase of Alaska, August 1, 1868] The deal was done! Many pages have been written about the existence of several checks of lesser amounts that may have gone to U.S. congressmen as bribes for their votes in Congress, and stories have been circulated concerning Stekl's withholding of some of the total funds for diplomatic payoffs to members of Congress. The notes of President Andrew Johnson also contain references to payments and a discussion between Johnson and Secretary of State Seward at the "old fields" seven or eight miles southeast of Washington on the "Road leading to Malsboro [Upper Marlboro] Md. on the 6th Sept Sundy 1868."[112] No clear information exists as to whether or not Stekl' gave payments to members of the U.S. Congress for their votes, nor how much he may have paid.

In 1869, Baron de Stekl' resigned due to ill-health and returned to St. Petersburg. Constantine de Catacazy, a secretary to the Russian legation for several years, remained in Washington and became Envoy Extraordinary and Minister Plentipotentiary, from 1869-1871.[113] Catacazy was described as a "wily, meddlesome intrieger who was poorly balanced for diplomatic service." He proved offensive to the U.S. This was during the first term of Ulyssus. S. Grant's presidency.[114]

The city directory for Washington recorded Catacazy as living at 1336 "I" (Eye) Street, NW. Waldemar de Bodisco was living at 149 West St. in Georgetown, and Boris Danzas was living at 1707 Pennsylvania Avenue, N.W. By the end of Catacazy's time in

Washington, the diplomatic legation had a military attache, General Alexandre Gorlow, who stayed three years (1871-73).[115]

Who was this difficult minister plenipotentiary, Constantine de Catacazy and how did his presence in Washington affect events between Russia and the U.S.? The U.S. was preparing in November 1871 for its first public royal visit from a European country, the Grand Duke of Russia, Alexis, third son of Emperor Alexander II, the Tsar Liberator of the serfs. The New York <u>Times</u> found it necessary to famililarize the American people with the personalities of the Russian Minister and his wife who would be at the center of many diplomatic receptions:

> Mr. Catacazy is . . . about fifty years of age. He was formerly attached to the Russian Legation in Washington as Chief Secretary, and it was while occupying that position that he formed the acquaintance of the French lady who subsequently became his wife. When he was accredited to this country as Minister Plenipotentiary, some of the diplomatic ladies in Washington refused, for reasons that do not concern the public, to be intimate with the family of the Minister. Smarting under this alleged unkind treatment, as it is said, he expressed his opinions, both by spoken and written words, in such decided terms that the President and his Cabinet took up the gauntlet, and in June last [1871] a letter was addressed to the Russian Government requesting the recall of Mr. Catacazy.[116]

The problems created by Constantine de Catacazy began as he "indirectly opposed" the work of the British and American "Joint High Commission" which was meeting on Franklin Square in Washington in the spring of 1871. The U.S. had accused Great Britain of fitting out Confederate ships in English ports and thereby prolonging the American Civil War by one or two years at a great expense to the budget of the U.S. Several members of President Grant's cabinet felt that the U.S. should seize Canada if Great Britain did not sign the *Alabama Treaty* and pay an indemnity of fifteen million dollars to the U.S. Catacazy directly approached U.S. senators to whom he spoke against the treaty's ratification and he urged a New York correspondent to write a newspaper article against the treaty.[117]

President Grant was so incensed by Catacazy's actions that he wrote to his Secretary of State, Hamilton Fish, that "it may be necessary to take some action towards the removal of the Russian Minister if he should not be recalled by his Govt." "My judgment is that he should be presented with his *walking papers* by our Govt." (Sept. 10, 1871).[118]

President Grant's wishes were tempered by diplomatic necessity. The U.S. did send a request to the Russian government, but the Russians were slow to respond. Grand Duke Alexis had scheduled a visit to the U.S. and was about to sail from St. Petersburg. If the Russian Emperor were forced to recall the Russian minister, would not the visit of Russia's Prince have to be abandoned also, sending chills through the relations of these two great countries? A deal was reached in which nothing would interrupt Prince Alexis' tour to the U.S. Only when the Prince finished his tour would Catacazy be excluded from his diplomatic functions: "his passports will be transmitted when this Government [U.S.] shall consider the visit of His Imperial Highness the Grand Duke Alexis as concluded."[119] The U.S., furthermore, did nothing to shorten the Prince's tour. At Emperor Alexander's personal request, Catacazy was "tolerated," but President Grant would only receive Catacazy when the Russian minister was in the presence of the Prince. The U.S. would offer "no salutes or other honours" to Catacazy which would normally be paid to a minister of a foreign government.[120]

The Grand Duke Alexis Alexandrovich, born in 1850, the fourth son of Emperor Alexander II, arrived in New York City on Nov. 20, 1871, and visited the White House in Washington on Nov. 23rd at 1 p.m., beginning a three-months tour to the U.S. that lasted until his departure on Feb. 23, 1872.[121]

Perhaps, it was Madame de Catacazy, a beautiful woman and wife of the Russian Minister, who also caused diplomatic coolness, for it was rumored that she had appeared in Washington several years before "when she had eloped from her [first] husband under the protection of Monsieur de Catacazy, then Secretary of the Russian Legation." It was also rumored that a "little Frenchwoman" had been employed in the Russian Legation through "the sympathies of its handsome mistress." This woman was given the run of the house and knew all the confidential communiques of the legation. All the public and private papers passed her eyes. Every day, she "made a written report of what she had heard and seen, which was privately sent to the Department of State, and for which she was . . . remunerated from the Secret Service Fund."[122]

Following Grand Duke Alexis' reception at the White House, he was handsomely "welcomed at the Russian Legation by Madame de Catacazy, who wore a dress of gold-colored silk, with a flowing train, elaborately trimmed with gold-colored satin. On her right arm she wore a double bracelet, one band being on the wrist and the other above the elbow, the two joined together by elaborately wrought chains. Her other ornaments were of plain gold, and above them was a wealth of golden hair."

"As the Grand Duke entered the Legation, Madame de Catacazy carried a silver salver, on which was placed a round loaf of black bread, on the top of which was imbedded a golden salt-cellar. The Prince took the uninviting loaf, broke and tasted of it, in accordance with the old Russian custom."[123]

"Eating Bread and Salt," [Grand Duke Alexis and Madame de Catacazy]. From Ben[jamin] Perley Poore, *Perley's Reminiscences of sixty years in the National Metropolis* (Philadelphia: Hubbard Brothers, 1886), vol. 2, p. 277.

THE GRAND DUKE ALEXIS.

"The Grand Duke Alexis." From Ben[jamin] Perley Poore, *Perley's Reminiscences*, p. 276.

The Grand Duke Alexis was received royally in the U.S. He visited 34 cities, hunted on the western prairies, shot buffalo with General Sheridan, hunted with General Custer and a troop of Sioux Indians, hunted with Buffalo Bill Cody, and visited New Orleans with General and Mrs. Custer at Mardi gras. The Grand Duke later rode from St. Louis, Missouri, to North Platte, Nebraska, "in a special five car train of new Pullman cars sumptuously outfitted." He visited Chicago shortly after the great fire of October 8-10, 1871, and gave $5,000 in gold to help the homeless people of that city.[124]

To commemorate Alexis' visit to the North American shores, Oliver Wendell Holmes wrote two poems to be delivered in song and readings at the Boston Music Hall and at the banquet on December 9, 1871:

> Welcome, thrice welcome! But not as a stranger, / Come to the nation that calls thee its friend!
>
> . . . .
>
> Throbbing and warm are the hearts that remember / Who was our friend when the world was our foe.
>
> . . . .
>
> How we utter *Farewell*, he will have to return![125]

Back in Washington, President Grant was preparing his "Annual Message" to Congress, dated December 4, 1871. The president wrote:

> "The intimate friendly relations which have so long existed between the United States and Russia continue undisturbed. . . . The inexcusable course of the Russian minister at Washington rendered it necessary to ask his recall, and to decline to longer receive that functionary as a diplomatic representative. It was impossible with self-respect, or with a just regard to the dignity of the country,

to permit Mr. Catacazy to continue to hold intercourse with this Government after his personal abuse of Government officials, and during his persistent interference, through various means, with the relations between the United States and other powers. In accordance with my wishes, this Government has been relieved of further intercourse with Mr. Catacazy, and the management of the affairs of the imperial legation has passed into the hands of a gentleman entirely unobjectionable."[126]

George Armstrong Custer, reclining in buckskinhunting outfit with rifle, Grand Duke Alexis seated beside him holding puppy." Photo by Scholten, [1872]. Library of Congress Prints and Photographs Division, Washington, DC. LC Bookmark: http/www.log.gov/pictures/item/2016646390/

"The Russian bear and the American dears." *Harper's Weekly* (Dec. 23, 1871), p. 1216. Library of Congress Prints and Photographs Division, Washington, DC. LC Bookmark: http://www.loc.gov/pictures/item/2002707008/

It was up to Boris Danzas, First Secretary of the Legation, and General Alexandre Gorloff, Military Attache, to hold together the Russian Legation until Baron d'Offenburg arrived in 1872.[127]

This new minister went by the name of Le Chevalier, Baron Henri d'Offenburg [Генрих Генрихович Оффенберг] and he served in Washington from 1872-75. He lived first at 1715 "H" Street, NW, and then at 1833 "G" Street, NW. Baron Offenburg was absent for a period in 1875, and Nicolas de Voigt served as Secretary of the Legation and interim Minister.[128] Baron Offenburg was a minor diplomat and is remembered for his earlier work in Europe in December of 1857 through April 1858 when he represented the Russian Empire at the "European Commission of the Danube" that delt with issues of canals and international shipping on the Danube River as required by the Peace of Paris of March 1856. In 1876, Nicholas Shishkin was appointed Minister and served until 1880. The several members of the Russian Legation lived in this same North West quadrant of Washington, at 1801 F Street, at 1804 Pennsylvania Avenue, 1017 Connecticut Avenue, and at 1736 "N" Street.[129]

By May of 1878, Shishkin was residing at the Clarendon Hotel in New York City and in poor health, having "given up his residence" in Washington. The Russian Minister wanted to be in New York City and closer to the shipping lanes to Europe in case war broke out between Russia and Great Britain at the end of the Russo-Turkish War of 1877-78. After his return to his homeland, Shishkin would go on to be Foreign Minister of the Russian Empire from 1896-97, following the death of Alexei Lobanov-Rostovsky, who served in that office for one year, 1895-96.[130]

From 1880-82, Michael Bartholomei [Михаил Федорович Бартоломей, 1836-95] lived in the Russian Legation house at 1015 Connecticut Avenue, NW, and attended the International Sanitary Conference of Washington in January of 1881 to represent his government. The delegates assembled to consider a system of notification "as to the actual sanitary conditions of ports and places . . . and of vessels sailing therefrom." Bartholomei was Russia's minister at the time of Emperor Alexander II's assassination and served briefly under Alexander III.[131]

Baron von Struve was appointed by Emperor Alexander III and served for a decade. The Struve family was well educated and came from both Denmark and Germany. In the early 19th century, sons of the Struve family were sent to the Estonian portion of the Russian Empire to avoid being conscripted into the Napoleonic army. They became scientists—mathematicians, astronomers, chemists, and government officials in Siberia, Perm, and Astrakhan on the Volga River.[132] Karl von Struve [Курилл Васильевич Струвь,1835-1907] had been assigned to Japan before being sent to Washington and the Legation at 1705 "K" Street, NW.[133] Marian Hooper Adams, who lived on Lafayette Square, wrote on Sunday, April 30, 1882, that the "new Russian Minister came in to tea a few days ago, has been to Japan for several years; his wife [Maria Nikolaevna Annenkova, 1844-89] has made a collection there of teapots—nine hundred and seventy-three so far—and has sent them to St. Petersburg, I'm sorry to hear." "She and I have exchanged calls but not met." "She is well-born and a lady, it is said, and will, it is hoped, atone for the shortcomings of her predecessors .[134]

Baron von Struve was able to represent Russia at the International Meridian Conference held in Washington in October 1884. The conference was held at the request of President Chester A. Arthur to choose "a meridian to be employed as a common zero of longitude and standard of time reckoning throughout the world." Struve was accompanied at the conference by Maj.-Gen. Stebnitzik of the Imperial Russian staff and M. J. de Kologrivoff, Conseiller d'Etat actual. The conference established Greenwich Mean Time for the entire world, and with four time zones for the Continental U.S.[135]

Maria Struve became ill and returned to Russia in 1885, where she died at Kielmarky, near St. Petersburg in 1889. From 1887-90, her husband Baron von Struve was absent from Washington. During these difficult years Baron Roman Rosen was listed as charge d'affaires.[136]

At the time of Maria Struve's illness and death and the absence of the Russian Minister from Washington, European events were disturbing relationships between Russia and the U.S. Following a foolish train wreck near Borki in the region of Kherson on October 17, 1888, in which the Emperor and his family miraculously escaped injury, the Emperor and his advisors initiated many oppressions against the Jewish communities of the Russian Empire. In 1890, "Russia and Western Europe were filled with alarming rumors" that reported the curtailment of "commercial activities of the Jews" and the establishment of Jewish ghettos in the major cities of the Russian Empire. "The foreign press made a terrible outcry against these contemplated new acts of barbarism." Jews in England took the initiative when they organized a December 10th, 1890, meeting in London's Guildhall which was attended by over 2,000 people.[137]

In America, the U.S. House of Representatives adopted a resolution on August 20, 1890, requesting President Benjamin Harrison "to communicate to the House of Representatives . . . any information in his possession concerning the enforcement of proscriptive edicts against the Jews in Russia. . . ." In response, President Harrison did lay "before Congress all the correspondence and papers bearing on the Jewish question in Russia" [Executive Documents, No. 470, dated Oct. 1, 1890].[138]

The Department of State was flooded with protests against the Russian atrocities. During the 1880's, a wave of 200,000 Russian Jews had immigrated to the U.S. and "continued persecutions in Russia were bound to result in a large and sudden immigration which was not unattended with danger." The U.S. was suffering from an economic downturn and did not feel it could settle and employ so many European citizens. The U.S. government sent, in June 1891, two commissioners, Weber and Kempster, to Russia to visit major cities and to "gather carefully sifted documentary evidence of what was being perpetrated upon the Jews" in the Russian Empire.[139]

At the time when Russian and U.S. relations were ripping apart, when Jewish immigration to Argentina, Canada, the U.S., and to Palestine had increased remarkably, the Russian diplomatic appointments in Washington were suffering from family emergencies and weak temporary subordinate appointments. During 1891-92, over 100,000 emigrants left Russia for the U.S.[140]

One famous Russian also left his homeland at about the same time, but only for 25 days [April 26 – May 20, 1891]. Peter Ilyich Tchaikovsky left for a tour of the U.S. which included conserts in New York City, in Philadelphia and in Baltimore. He even had time to visit and view Niagara Falls. Tchaikovsky was present at the opening of the new Carnegie Hall in New York City.[141]

In his one overnight visit to Washington, he dined at the Metropolitan Club in the company of F. Hansen, Acting Secretary, Alexander Greger, 2nd Secretary of the Russian Legation at 1705 K Street, NW, and Botkin who accompanied him on the tour.[142] Following supper, Tchaikovsky was entertained at a gala for one hundred guests at the Legation House, across Farragut Square from the Metropolitan Club, at 10 o'clock in the evening. He was met then at the Legation House by Baron von Struve who had returned from a business trip to New York City just to receive Tchaikovsky. From Tchaikovsky's Diary we learn of this evening:

> The ambassador [minister] appeared. He turned out to be an old man, very cordial, simple in manner and in general extremely congenial. . . . Almost all the ladies spoke French . . . I was not especially burdened . . . . The program included my Trio [op. 50] and a quartet by Brahms [op. 25].
>
> The piano part was performed by Secretary Hansen, who seems to be quite a good pianist. He played my Trio extremely well. The violinist was rather poor. . . .
>
> After the music an excellent cold supper was served. After most of the guests had departed, ten of us . . . sat a long while at a big round table, sipping most perfect wine. Struve apparently enjoys very much to have an extra glass of wine. He gives the impression of a man, heartbroken and sad, seeking oblivion from his sorrows in wine.
>
> At about 3 o'clock I came home [Hotel Arlington], accompanied by Botkin and Hansen. Slept well.[143]

Tchaikovsky's last day in Washington [May 17, 1892] was a whirlwind sightseeing extravaganza: Tchaikovsky had tea after rising, strolled in the city [White House area ?] returned home [Arlington House ?] for a light nap, met Struve at noon for breakfast at the Metropolitan Club, took a tour of the city seeing the "famous obelisk," the Capitol, the Soldier's Home and park for veterans, returned to the Russian Legation, drank tea, chatted with Struve, played the legation piano with Hansen, and dined with the legation staff at the Metropolitan Club, and then departed the nation's capital for New York City. In May Tchaikovsky recorded that Washington was "buried in the dense luxurious foliage of chestnuts, acacias, oaks, and maples."[144]

Finally, in August of 1892, Baron von Struve was transferred to The Hague and succeeded in Washington by Prince Cantacuzene from the Russian Embassy at Vienna.[145]

Peter Ilich Tchaikovsky, Photographed by Vezenberg & Co., St. Petersburg, Russia, between 1880 and 1886. Library of Congress. LC-USZ62-128254 [reproduction number].

Grand Duke Alexander Mikhailovich of Russia (1866-1933). Library of Congress, LC-DIG-ggbain-16951 [reproduction number].

One other member of the Russian royal family visited Washington, in January of 1893 and again in 1913 for a return. This was Grand Duke Alexander Mikhaelovitch (1866-1934) who was a grandson of Nicholas I and a cousin of the present Emperor, Alexander III. Grand Duke Alexander also was in love with Xenia, who was the daughter of the Emperor and the Grand Duke's first cousin once removed. When the Grand Duke came in 1893, he sailed on Russia's newest cruiser *Dimitry Donskoi* with an official function "to thank the Americans for the help extended by them during the partial Russian famine" of the summer of 1892. Grand Duke Alexander was twenty-seven years old when his ship docked at Manhatten's New York City dock on the Hudson River. He came "to express to President Cleveland the gratitude of my imperial cousin, Czar Alexander III, for the help extended by the American nation during the Russian famine." He also wanted personally to get a taste of the future in such a new nation devoid of past traditions. The World's Fair was about to open in Chicago and the "whole country was sizzling with excitement":

> Russia possessed gold, ore, copper, coal, iron; its soil, if properly cultivated, should have been able to feed the whole world. What was the matter with us? Why did we not follow the American way of doing things? . . . I commenced working out a large plan for the Americanization of Russia.[146]

Over his early years, Grand Duke Alexander learned several lessons, especially the "advantages derived from the absence of frozen classes"—from a classless society that can approach issues in a new and creative manner.[147] In the summer of 1913 for his return visit, the Grand Duke left his wife and family at Xenia's family home in the Crimea and sailed again for America to investigate the advances in air flight being made by Glenn Hammond Curtiss and Wilbut and Orville Wright, America's aviation pioneers. After Russia's naval defeats to the Japanese in the 1904-06 Pacific war, Alexander turned his attention to air superiority. He also appreciated the building of the Panama Canal as a means for expansion into the Pacific Ocean. The U.S. was developing "a new piece of remarkable machinery" while central Europe was building "munition plants." The contrast between America and Europe was stark—America created a new energy, Europe produced war and destruction.[148] Such was the influence of the United States at that time.

Prince Gregory Cantacuzene [Грегорий Львович Кантакузен, 1843-1902] resided at the Legation at 1829 "I" Street, NW, in 1895 for a very short time.[149] Prince Cantacuzene had with him his young daughter, "who was very popular among the limited circle of acquaintances." Princess Cantacuzene was to make her debut in Russian society during the 1896 winter season and her father withdrew to St. Petersburg, Russia, in October of 1895, to make arrangement for her presentation. The couple "left the city so quietly . . . that not even . . . intimate friends had any knowledge of . . . intentions." It was said that the Prince "entertained a horror of formal farewells."[150]

The next appointment, Ernest de Kotzebue [Ёрнст Карлович Коцебу, 1834-1914], also lasted a short time. Once established in the city, Ambassador Ernest Kotzebue arranged to give a "moonlight fete in honor of the coronation of the czar [Nicholas II], May 25, 1896." It was to be an outside affair, with music, and a gorgeous display of fireworks. A newspaper writeup continued: "A feast characteristic of the banquets of the empire of the two continents will be spread." The paper also hinted that the ambassador's wife was following behind and was expected to arrive in the U.S. in time for "this unique demonstration of loyalty."[151] It was reported in Oct. 11, 1897, that the Russian Minister was in St. Petersburg on leave of absence and that he had decided not to return. His health is not so robust as when he first came to Washington."[152]

Mr. de Wollant [Vollant] was the Charge d'Affaires when Russia and the U.S. established embassy status in April 1898. No longer would there be envoys extraordinary and ministers plenipotentiary between these two large countries. It was a symbol that Europoen powers finally accepted the U.S. as an equal country.[153]

The first full-level ambassador from Russia to the U.S. was Arthur Paul Nicholas Cassini, Marquis de Cipizzucchi de Bologna, Count Cassini [Артупр Павлович Кассини], who served in the post from 1897-1905.[154] Count Cassini had both a naval and military agent in the embassy. Apparently, the ambassador lived at 1829 "I" Street, NW. "The Embassy is one of the fine old roomy mansions of Washington, without special pretense to architectural show." Count Cassini had begun his "distinguished career in Asia, and [was] one of the most astute diplomats in the world." He had a young girl presiding over the embassy," his grandniece, Margaret Cassini, "who had tea served from the samovar, after the Russian faction."[155]

"The Drawing-Room in the Russian Embassy, from Charles M. Pepper, *Every-Day Life in Washington: with pen and camera* (New York: The Christian Herald, Louis Klopsch, Proprietor, 1900), p. 213. [Location of the residence may have been at 1829 or 1634 "I" Street, NW, Washington, DC, during the 1890s.]

Sergei Witte, Baron Rosen with their suite and newspaper men [heavily cropped]. Library of Congress, LC-DIG-ppmsca-08804 [reproduction number].

This grand niece Margaret was known informally as "Maggie" and became a close personal friend of Alice Roosevelt, daughter of President Theodore Roosevelt, for "Maggie" was only too years older than Alice. Ever since "Maggie" Cassini arrived in Washington in 1898, when she was sixteen years of age, she was ordered by Count Cassini to take over the duties of official hostess of the Russian Embassy.[156]

A diplomat who had known Count Cassini in Asia described the Russian ambassador as one of the shrewdest and ablest of diplomats in the Russian service. It was said that for twelve years he had got the better of all the delegations in Pekin and controlled that extraordinary ruler of China, the dowager queen. Cassini told me that from his intimate associations with her he had formed the opinion that she was quite equal to Catherine of Russia, whom he regarded as the greatest woman sovereign who ever lived.[157]

Before being assigned to Washington, Count Cassini was "practically Viceroy of the Far East." When he moved through the streets of Peking, *sotnias* of Cossacks [сотня Казачья] dashed ahead and cleared the way for the little man [Cassini] with the monocle who for four years, with the dreaded power of Russia behind him, dominated four hundred million Chinese and made them do his bidding."[158] Cassini's Secretary of the Legation, Gregoire de Wollant, had also served in the Orient as Acting Consul from 1890-92 in Nagasaki, Japan.[159] (Following the Russian Revolution of 1917, a friend of Count Cassini recorded that he saw an elderly Cassini "so long ambassador extraordinary of Holy Russia, running through the sleet and rain on the Place de la Madeleine [Paris] to catch a bus to take him to the modest suburban retreat, or refuge which the French government [had] provided him."[160] No longer was there a Cossack squadron accompanying Cassini.

Being left in charge of the diplomatic entertainment of the embassy, "Maggie" Cassini spent her days dining with older men. When Theodore Roosevelt met her at an "inauguration" eve dinner in 1901, Roosevelt remarked, "It is Anna Karenina!" "Why Anna

Karenina, Colonel Roosevelt?" the beautiful hostess asked. "There is tragedy in your eyes," he answered.[161]

Some folk in high circles of society thought Count Cassini "even more pompous than his full name suggested" and they would "grow to despise the very sight of him." When he arrived and after "Maggie" arrived in 1898, this "budding beauty at his side was introduced to society as the daughter of [Count Cassini's] dead brother." Later, Count Cassini returned to Russia "to adopt the girl." "According to a rumor, the count had no need to adopt Maggie, as she had always been his daughter—by his housekeeper." When Countess Cassini wrote her memoirs, she explained that her mother had been a singer in the theatre. "Because the czar would never have consented to the marriage of one of his diplomats to a singer, the count [married] secretly and ordered the child of this marriage to pretend that her mother was her governess."[162] (The maternal grandson of Count Cassini, Oleg Cassini Loiewski, born in Paris in 1913, was a designer to Jacqueline Kennedy and created the new image for the First Lady, which became the first memorable fashion line to emerge on television and included the pillbox hat.)[163]

Several major historical events occurred during the period of Count Cassini that disturbed the Americans: the massacre of about 100 Jews in Kischineff, the capital of Moldova, in 1902, the Russo-Japanese War, and first revolution of 1905-06. In a newspaper article, Count Cassini explained "the conditions of the Jews in Russia and the provocation for the peasants' hatred." "Cassini explained that the peasants were against the money-lenders and not the Russian public against the Jews." The Russian government will "take measures to punish the guilty persons implicated in the massacres at Kischineff, Moldova." On the other hand, the U.S. Department of State refused "to discuss the possibililty of interference by the U.S. on behalf of the Jews."[164]

The ambassador also pointed out that he resented the "slander" against Russia that was printed in American newspapers: "Disturbances among the [Russian] university students last March . . . were no worse than they usually are." "Russian students are like the students of America and every other country." "They are merely boys full of vitality, which sometimes expresses itself in reckless and lawless form. . . ." "At no time did they amount to a serious demonstration against the government, and at no time were the students supported by the workingmen of St. Petersburg or elsewhere."[165]

Cassini, as a character on stage, even turns up in a children's musical, *Teddy Roosevelt and the Treasure of Ursa Major*, by Tom Isbell with songs by satirist Mark Russell (musical 2006, book 2008).[166]

Baron Roman Rosen [Роман Романович Розен, 1847-1921] who replaced Cassini, had served as ambassador to the Japanese Empire, from 1905-1911,[167] during Russia's critical years in Asia. The Rosens were a Baltic German family with a Swedish title. One of his ancestors had been an outstanding Russian commander at the Battle of Borodino, September 7, 1812. Baron Rosen had received a diplomatic education and began his career in the Balkans, moved to Mexico, Serbia, and finally a short year in Japan before being sent to the U.S. He concluded the Nishi-Rosen Agreement between Russia and Japan which softened the dispute over Korea and established Russian dominance in Manchuria.

Baron Rosen was in Tokyo at the start of the Russo-Japanese War (1905) and was sent by Emperor Nicholas II as the new Russian ambassador to the U.S. to assist Sergei Witte at the Portsmouth, New Hampshire, negotiations which President Theodore Roosevelt had convened to work out a "cessation of hostilities" and a lasting peace. The Portsmouth Treaty contained "favorable terms for Russia." Rosen was recalled to St. Petersburg in 1911 and was appointed to the State Council of Imperial Russia until the overthrow of the monarchy by the February Revolution of 1917. As the Revolution progressed, Rosen and his family escaped to Sweden and then to the U.S. He wrote a series of articles about European diplomacy and politics for *The Saturday Evening Post*, including "Forty Years of a Diplomat's Life," that ran from 1919 through 1921.[168]

During his ambassador days in Washington, Baron Rosen resided in the Russian Legation at 1634 "I" Street, NW. At his death in 1921, Rosen was buried on Lot 516 (East) in Georgetown's Oak Hill Cemetery.[169]

In 1917, the Russian Foreign Office sent George Bakhmeteff [Георгий Юрий Петрович Бахметев, 1848-1928] to Washington to replace Baron Rosen. Bakhmeteff was from a diplomatic family of Tatar nobles who had converted to the Russian Orthodix faith. Before Bakhmeteff came to Washington he had been assigned as Russian Ambassador to Japan.[170] He served in the U.S. from November 1911 through March 1917. During his stay in Washington, Bakhmeteff lived at 1634 "I" Street, NW, and then at 1517 "L" Street, NW.[171]

George Baklmeteff standing alongside carriage on which his wife [Maria] is seated, with dog [and driver]. Library of Congress, LC-USZ62-126978 [reproduction number]. Copyrighted by Clinedinst, Washington, ED, about 1912.

Boris [and Helen] Bakhmeteff. Created May 13, 1922. Library of Congress, LC-DIG-npcc-06345 [reproduction number].

Bakhmeteff married the daughter of a Washington social couple, Mary Beale. In a sense, Bakhmeteff's assignment to the U.S. was a homecoming for him and his wife Mary [Maria] Beale. She had been born in Chester, Pennsylvania, the daughter of General Edward Fitzgerald Beale. Edward F. Beale had been appointed a minister to the Austria-Hungary capital of Vienna in 1876. Mary [Maria] Beale went with her father to Vienna and married a Russian diplomat, in 1877, whom she had met previously in Washington the year before when George Bakhmeteff had served as a young 2nd Secretary of the Russian Legation and lived at 1804 Pennsylvania Avenue, NW. Mary Beale's brother served also as an ambassador in Europe and her sister was the wife of the publisher of the Washington <u>Post</u>, John Roll McLean.[172]

After their marriage, George and Maria Bakhmeteff were assigned to Greece and then Bulgaria. During the troubles in Macedonia, Maria Bakhmeteff "threw open her home to refugees." For her charitable work, Madame Bakhmeteff was decorated by the rulers of Russia, Bulgaria, Rumania and the Sultan of Turkey. With the assignment to Washington in 1911, the couple "entertained lavishly for their friends." "Mme, Bakhmeteff's good taste and tact made her one of the most popular hostesses of the diplomatic set" and her "collection of jewels, containing an unusual number of exquisite uncut rubies, was the admiration of young Washington matrons, and she had the reputation of being one of the best-dressed women of an embassy celebrated for the appearance of its members."[173]

Quite tangential to the new Russian Ambassador and his marriage, the wealthy widow of George Pullman, Hattie Sanger Pullman, commissioned the construction of an urban mansion on North 16th Street, NW, for the use of Pullman's daughter and her son-in-law congressman. The architect was Nathan Wyeth who was in Washington "overseeing the expansion of the West Wing of the White House." Mrs. Pullman and her family members did not live in the mansion which was then sold in 1913 to the Russian Government for a sum of $350,000 [dollars].[174]

Ambassador and Mrs. Bakhmeteff were the first Russian diplomats to live in the mansion at 1119 16th Street, NW, where they "impressed

Washington society with their elaborate entertaining" until the 1917 Revolution.[175] The Pullman Mansion / Embassy was taken over by the Kerensky provisional government from 1917 through 1922, when the mansion stood vacant until the U.S. recognition of the Soviet Union in 1934.[176]

In 1917, when the Bakhmeteffs left Washington following the abdication of the czarist government in Russia, they may have taken furnishings from the embassy building to Paris.

Boris Bakhmeteff [Борис Александрович Бахметев, 1880-1951] was a mechanical and hydraulics engineer who represented the Provisional Government of Kerensky to the U.S. from his arrival in June 1917 until the U.S. ended its recognition of that government in 1922. Boris and his wife Helen were unrelated to the former Ambassador George Bakhmeteff. Boris became a professor of Civil Engineering at Columbia University in New York City. Following the 1922 end of his ambassadorship and the 1921 death of his wife Helen, he established the Lion Match Company with other Russian immigrants.[177] The Archives of Russian History and Culture in the Rare Books & Manuscript Library (Butler Library) of the Columbia University Libraries were established by Boris Bakhmeteff.[178]

From the Decatur House to the Pullman House, from Georgetown's parlors to grass and tree covered lots in Oak Hill Cemetery, from official dinners and receptions in the Presidential Mansion to an impromptu visit to Monticello or an excursion to Niagara Falls and Auburn, New York, the distinguished ministers and ambassadors of the Russian Empire attached themselves to the hearts of social Washington as did the Soviet sailors attach themselves to the citizens of Gloucester in the humorous and fictitious movie *The Russians Are Coming*. Throughout a century, from the 1810's to the 1920's and social revolution, the presence of Imperial Russia found a home (and their ministers found several American wives) in the diplomatic post of Washington, D.C. The assignment was not all work as the social amenities took precedence. Two great countries on the rise, with very different histories, managed to retain an harmonious relationship, to the advantage of both countries.

NOTES

1   United Artists, 1966.

2   *The United States and Russia: the Beginning of Relations, 1765-1815*, eds. N. N. Bashkina, et al. (Joint Soviet American Editorial Board, 1976-1979), pp. 33-35.

3   Nicholas V. Riasanovsky, *A History of Russia*, 2d. ed. (N.Y.: Oxford University Press, 1969), pp. 287-289; and "Pugachev's Rebellion," Wikipedia, the free encyclopedia.

4   *The United States and Russia*, N. N. Bashkina, pp. 99-101.

5   Mary Claffey and Sara Sikes, "The First Ambassador: John Quincy Adams in St. Petersburg, 1809-1815, *Russian Life* (Sept. / Oct. 2008), p. 50.

6   *The United States and Russia*, N. N. Bashkina, pp. 254-256.

7   Emperor Paul I, 1796-1801, was murdered on March 11 os [23 ns], 1801; Nathaniel Christopher, "Russia's Distant American Shore," *Russian Life* (May / June 2008), p. 54.

8   *The United States and Russia*, N. N. Bashkina, pp. 521-526.

9   Garry Wills, *Henry Adams and the Making of America* (Boston: Houghton Mifflin, 2005), p. 244; *The United States and Russia*, N. N. Bashkina, p. 1125.

10   Ibid., pp. 576-585.

11   Ibid., p. 583.

12   Ibid., p. 747; *The Papers of Thomas Jefferson: Retirement Series (1811)* (Princeton: Princeton University Press, 1950-), Vol. 3, pages 532, 539, 563, and 567.

13   Harry Ammon, *James Monroe: the Quest for National Identity* (N.Y.: McGraw-Hill, 1971), p. 319; David W. McFadden, "John Quincy Adams, American Commercial Diplomacy, and Russia 1809-1825," in *The New England Quarlerly*, Vol. 66, No. 4 (Dec. 1993), pp. 613-629.

14   S. Somervell Mackall, *Early Days of Washington* (Washington: The Neale Company, 1899) (reprint ed.: Sterling, Illinois:G. E. Bishop Printing Co., 1934), Chapter X, pp. 114-123.

15   George Washington Parke Custis, oration, *The Celebration of the Russian Victories, in Georgetown, District of Columbia; on the 5ᵗʰ of June, 1813*

(Georgetown, D.C.: Printed by J. B. Carter, 1813). The Oration of Mr. Custis and the address of Mr. Harper are included.

16 Robert Goodloe Harper moved from Charleston, SC, to Baltimore, Md., and married in 1800 Catherine Carroll of Anne Arundel County, Md. He served as a major general in the War of 1812 and was elected to the U.S. Senate from Maryland in 1816.

17 High Beam Encyclopedia, 1997, copyrighted by Daniel L. Schlafly, Jr.

18 The United States and Russia, N. N. Bashkina, pp. 1089 and 1097.

19 Steven A. Usitalo and William Benton Whisenhunt, Russian and Soviet History: from the Time of Troubles to the Collapse of the Soviet Union (Lanham, Mass.: Rowan & Littlefield, 2008), p. 116.

20 Ibid., p. 117; "Kozlov Affair (1815)" in High Beam Encyclopedia, 1997, copyrighted by Daniel L. Schlafly, Jr.; Harry Ammon, James Monroe: the Quest for National Identity (N.Y.: McGraw-Hill, 1971), p. 350.

21 Washington Directory, comp. by Judah Delano (Washington: William Duncan, 1822).

22 Petr Poletika's book, A Sketch of the Internal Conditions of the USA and their Political Relations with Europe, was written in the USA in 1810-22, and published in Paris and Baltimore by E. J. Coale, in 1826. It contained 163 pages.

23 Baron Van Tuyll was born in 1771 in Zuylen, Holland, of a Dutch noble family. He became a major general in the Russian Army and opposed Napoleon's invasion of his adopted land. Later, he worked his way up in the Russian diplomatic corps to become a Minister Plentipotentiary to the U.S. See: website: Тейль ван Сераскеркен, Фёдор Васильвич.

24 Suzanne Massie, Land of the Firebird: the Beauty of Old Russia (N.Y.: Simon & Schuster/Touchstone, 1980, pap. 1982), p. 159.

25 Rufus Rockwell Wilson, Washington, the Capital City, Vol. I (Philadelphia: J. B. Lippincott, 1902), p. 182; Harold Donaldson Eberlein and Courtland VanDyke Hubbard, Historic Houses of George-Town & Washington City (Richmond, VA: Dietz Press, Incorporated, 1938).

26 Paul E. Richardson, "Colonial Russia," Russian Life (Sept. / Oct. 2007), Vol. 50, No. 5, pp. 48-51; Steve Moyer, "Russian Dreams of an American Colony: Fort Ross," Humanities: the magazine of the National Endowment for the Humanities (March / April 2012), Vol. 33, No. 2, pp. 28-31, 51.

27 W. P. Cresson, The Holy Alliance: the European Background of the Monroe Doctrine (N.Y.: Oxford University Press, 1922), p. 51.

28 Nathaniel Christopher, "Russia's Distant American Shore," Russian Life (May / June 2008), Vol. 51, No. 3, pp. 54; Irby C. Nichols, Jr., "The Russian Ukase and the Monroe Doctrine: a Re-evaluation," The Pacific Historical Review, Vol. 36, No. 1 (Feb., 1967), pp. 13-26.

29 Ibid.

30 Records of Boundary and Claims Commissions and Arbitrations, 1716-1979, RG 76, Entry 360, U.S. National Archives, College Park, Md., "Memorandum on the 1825 Boundary Line between British and Russian Possessions in North American. . . ."

31 Nicholas V. Riasanovsky, A History of Russia, 2d ed. (N.Y.: Oxford University Press, 1969), p. 352; Daniel Walker Howe, "Monroe Doctrine," in What Hath God Wrought: the Transformation of America, 1815-1848 (Oxford, 2007, pap. 2009), pp. 111-117.

32 Allen Johnson, "Ch. XIV-Framing an American Policy," in Jefferson and His Colleagues: a Chronicle of the Virginia Dynasty (Chronicles of American Series; 15) (New Haven: Yale University Press, 1921), pp. 286-307.

33 Michael Bednar, L'Enfant's Legacy: Public Open Spaces in Washington, D.C. (Baltimore: The Johns Hopkins University Press, 2006), p. 97.

34 Washington, D.C.: a Turn-of-the-Century Treasury, ed. by Frank Oppel & Tony Meisel (Secaucus, N.J.: Castle, 1987), p. 17.

35 Suzanne Massie, Land of the Firebird: the Beauty of Old Russia (N.Y.: Simon & Schuster, 1980, paper 1982), p. 269-270.

36 The Papers of Henry Clay, ed. by Hames F. Hopkins and Mary W. M. Hargreaves, Vol. 5-Secretary of State, 1826 (Lexington: University Press of Kentucky, 1959-), pp. 205-207; Julie Kowalsky, "Decatur House," in Guiding Light (in-house magazine of the Decatur House).

37 John Quincy Adams, Memoirs, Vol. 6 (Philadelphia: J. B. Lippincott, 1875), pp. 453-454.

38 Joan M. Dixon, comp., National Intelligencer, Newspaper Abstracts, 1824-1826 (Bowie, Md.: Heritage Books, 1999), p. 334 [May 1, 1826, Monday].

39 Ibid., p. 339 [May 11, 1826, Thursday].

40 Ibid., p. 337 [May 4, 1826, Thursday].

41 Information supplied by Jarod Kearney, Curator, James Monroe Museum and Memorial Library, Fredericksburg, Virginia; Hans Huth, "White House Furniture at the Time of Monroe," Gazette Des Beaux Arts, Vol. 29 (January 1946), 24-25; William G. Allman and Melixsa C. Naulin, Something of Splendor: Decoratie Arts from the White House: an exhibit at the Renwick Gallery of the Smithsoniam American Art Museum, Oct. 1, 2011 to May 6, 2012 (Washington: Office of the Curator, White House, 2011), pp. 24-25.

42 "Notes from the Russian Legation to the U.S. Department of State, 1809-1906," Record Group 59, Roll 2 (April 12, 1826-Dec. 11, 1849), U.S. National Archives, College Park, Md., Entry for August 20, 1826 / Sept. 1, 1826, on Roll 2.

43 U.S. National Archives, Record Group 217, Microfilm 235 publication, case number 70467 (August 10, 1836), from the Miscellaneous Treasury Accounts

of the First Auditor, 1790-1840. The note reads: "Office, Bank, U States, Washington, June 29, 1833—By direction of Baron Krudener I have this day delivered, to Mr. [Geo W] South, two cases of silver plate, containing the several articles corresponding as near as I could ascertain with the written invoice. . . ." Earlier accounts incorrectly associated the silver purchases with the Thomas Jefferson administration. "Jefferson's White House Inventory," in <u>Antiques</u> (Boston, Mass.), Vol. 15 (June 1929), pp. 485-486; and Abby G. Baker, "The White House Collection of Presidential Ware," in <u>The Century Magazine</u> (May – October, 1908), Vol. 76, n.s., Vol. 54, p. 833-834. The Papers of Andrew Jackson Project in Knoxville, Tennessee, confirmed the case number from the U. S. First Auditor's file, # 70467, in the National Archives, R.G. 217, Microfilm 235, for August 10, 1836.

44 "Henry Walker Dead," in The Washington <u>Post</u>, Nov. 24, 1901; ProQuest Historical Newspapers The Washington <u>Post</u> (1877-1992) p. 2.

45 <u>Lippincott's Magazine of Popular Literature and Science</u>, Vol. 12, no. 31 (October 1873); and "Russia's First Iron Road," ed. by Tamara Eidelman, in "Russian Calendar," in <u>Russian Life</u>, Vol. 55, no. 5 (September/October 2012), pp. 23-24.

46 Alexis de Tocqueville, <u>Democracy in America</u>, Vol. I (N.Y.: 1835), pp. 395-396.

47 Philip Shriver Klein, <u>President James Buchanan: a Biography</u> (University Park, Pennsylvania: Pennslyvania State University, 1962), pp. 81-82.

48 Ibid., p. 88.

49 Ibid., p. 89.

50 Ibid., pp. 89-90.

51 "Notes from the Russian Legation in the U.S. to the Department of State, 1809-1906," Record Group 59, op. cit., Roll 1. On May 2, 1838, Mr. Bodisco was received by the U.S. Secretary of State Forsyth. See also: Sally Somervell Mackall, <u>Early Days of Washington</u> (Washington: Neale Co., 1899, rep. 1934), p. 327.

52 "A Russian Count's Family: Death of Waldemar de Bodisco at Jordan Allum Springs," in The Washington <u>Post</u> (1877-1954); Aug. 3, 1878; ProQuest Historical Newspapers The Washington <u>Post</u> (1877-1992), p. 1.

53 Mackall, op. cit., pp. 311-328.

54 Ibid., pp. 311-319.

55 Robert Reed, <u>Old Washington, D.C., in early photographs, 1846-1932</u> (N.Y.: Dover Publications, Inc., 1980), pp. 156-157. This Clement Smith House, at 3322 "O" Street, N.W. in Georgetown, was built in 1815. From 1838 to 1854 the home belonged to Alexander, Baron de Bodisco, Russian Ambassador to Washington. During the Civil War the house bacame a headquarters for Union officers. It was later subdivided and rended as apartments. The Hon.

John and Mrs. Teresa Keery greatly restored the home, when it became known as the Heinz-Kerry Home. See also: Addendum to Bodisco House (Clement Smith House) 3322 O Street, Northwest, Washington, D.C., Historic American Buildings Survey, HABS DC-174, DC Geo, 38.

56 Crestwood was bought by Alexander de Bodisco. See: Crestwood Community Organization on the Web. The Bodisco home stood at the corner of 18th and Varnum Streets until the 1930's. The estate was between 16th Street NW and Rock Creek, and the area still has the name of Crestwood Community.

57 Daniel Walker Howe, What Hath God Wrought: the Transformation of America, 1815-1848 (N.Y.: Oxford University Press, 2007, paper 2009), pp. 706-707.

58 The Washington Directory, and National Register, for 1846, comp. by Gaither & Addison (Washington: John T. Towers, 1846), "Russia," p. 27.

59 Ibid., "Russia," p. 55.

60 Klein, op. cit., p. 171.

61 Allen Cullins Clark, Life and Letters of Dolly [sic] Madison (Washington, DC: W. F. Roberts Company, 1914), p. 376, and Esther Singleton's The Story of the White House (NY: McClure Co., 1907), 2 Vols. See also: Kalorama, Washington, D.C. – Wikipedia, the free encyclopedia; and, E. G. Arnold, Topographical Map of the Original District of Columbia . . . (N.Y.: G. Woolworth Colton, 1862; reprinted Washington: A. W. K. Design, 1981).

62 Richard F. Grimmett, St. John's Church, Lafayette Square: the history and heritage of the church of the presidents, Washington, D.C. (Minneapolis, MN: Mill City Press, Inc., 2009), pp. 61-64 and footnotes on pp. 284-285.

63 Alexander de Bodisco, 1855, Probate, District of Columbia, found in the U.S. National Archives, Pennsylvania Avenue, D.C., Record Group 21, Entry 115, Number 3500 O.S.—"1856 account of the Executors of the late Alex de Bodisco Estate."

64 Ibid., "The first and final account of Brooke B. Williams as Collector of the Estate of the late M. Alexander de Bodisco.

65 "Obituary 1, The Washington Post (1877-1954); Aug. 3, 1878; ProQuest Historical Newspapers The Washington Post (1877-1992) p. 4. and "A Russian Funeral," The Washington Post (1877-1954); Aug. 5, 1878; ProQuest Historical Newspapers The Washington Post (1877-1992) p. 1.

66 Ibid.

67 Waldemar De Bodisco, Probate Records, District of Columbia, U.S. National Archives, Pennsylvania Avenue, DC, Record Group 21, Entry 115, Number OS 8340. Statement, Georgetown, D.C., July 1878, to Mr. Waldemar de Bocisco for sons Masters Alexr Boris & Waldr, To The President and Directors of Georgetown College, DC.

68   Frank A. Golder, "The American Civil War Through the Eyes of a Russian Diplomat," in The American Historical Review, Vol. 26, no. 3 (April 1921), pp. 454–463; Boyd's Washington and Georgetown Directory. . . 1860, comp. by William H. Boyd (Washington, DC: Taylor and Maury, 1860), Appendix, under "Russia."

69   A. A. Woldman, Lincoln and the Russians (Cleveland: World Pub. Co., 1952), pp. 1-14.

70   Ibid.; and Susanne Sternthal, "The Curious Entente Cordial: President Lincoln and Tsar Alexander II," in Russian Life, Vol. 55, no. 4 (July/August 2012), p. 40.

71   Frank A. Golder, "Russian-Anerican Relations during the Crimean War," in The American Historical Review, Vol. 31, no. 3 (April 1926), p. 476.

72   "Eduard Andreevich Stoeckl," in Wikipedia, the free encyclopedia; "Eduard Stekl," in SpeedyLook encyclopedia.

73   A. A. Woldman, op. cit., pp. 15-16.

74   Harrison E. Salisbury, War Between Russia and China (N.Y.: W. W. Norton, 1969), pp. 59-60.

75   Philip Shriver Klein, op. cit., p. 272; A. A.Woldman, op. cit., p. 18.

76   A. A. Woldman, op. cit., pp. 25, 41, 45 and 47.

77   Susanne Sternthal, op. cit., pp. 38-45.

78   Colton's Map of the World (N.Y.: J. H. Colton & Co., [1855]), with annotations by Mr. Collins. "Mr. Collins; Proposed Overland Pacific Telegraph, San Francisco to Moscow." [St. Louis—San Francisco—Alaska [Russian America]—Tchuktchi—Okhotsk—Amur River—Irkoutsk—Tomsk—with lines to Peking and Tokyo and east coast of Korea—Kazan—Nijnii Novgorod—Moscow—from Kazan south to Astrachan and Teheran (Persia).] This Colton's Map may be located in the U.S.National Archives, Pennsylvania Avenue, Washington, D.C., under "Map showing overland Pacific Telegraph from San Francisco to Moscow, submitted to the Committee on Commerce with a petition for a survey for a telegraphic line from the Amoor River to Russian America, ca. 1862." Maps and Charts from the U.S. House of Representatives, Committee on Commerce (1819-1892), Center for Legislative Archives, Washington, D.C., Item from Record Group 233, Records of the U.S. House of Representatives, 1789-2006. NAIL Control Number: NWL-233-PETITIONCOM-37AG28-1.

79   Frank A. Golder, "The Russian Fleet and the Civil War," in The American Historical Review, Vol. 20, no. 4 (July 1915), pp. 801-812.

80   A. A. Woldman, op. cit., p. 161.

81   Marshall B. Davidson, "A Royal Welcome for the Russian Navy," American Heritage, Vol. 11, no. 4 (June 1960), p. 38; Thurlow Weed, Memoir of Thurlow Weed, Vol. II (Boston: Houghton Mifflin, 1884), pp. 346-347.

82 "Our Naval Visitors: The Russian Fleet in the Harbor, Sketches of the Vessels, Officers. Etc." New York Times (Sept. 26, 1863), fron ProQuest Historical Newspapers: New York Times (1851-2009), p. 5; "Sergius of Radonezh, born c. 1314," in Russian Life (May / June 2009), p. 25.

83 Suzanne Massie, Land of the Firebird: the Beauty of Old Russia (New York: Simon & Schuster, Touchstone Book, 1980), pp. 352-353.

84 The Tsar and the President: Alexander II and Abraham Lincoln, Liberator and Emancipator, ed. by Marilyn Pfiefer Swezey (Washington, DC: American-Russian Cultural Cooperation Foundation, 2008), p. 41.

85 "Our Russian Guests," New York Times (Oct. 4, 1863), in ProQuest Historical Newspapers: The New York Times (1851-2009), p. 8.

86 "Our Russian Visitors," New York Times (Sept. 29, 1863), in ProQuest Historical Newspapers: The New York Times (1851-2009), p. 4.

87 "Our Russian Guests," New York Times (Oct. 4, 1863), in ProQuest Historical Newspapers: The New York Times (1851-2009), p. 8.

88 "The Russian Padre," New York Times (Sept. 27, 1863), in ProQuest Historical Newspapers: The New York Times (1851-2009), p. 5.

89 "Ihr Russian Guests," under "Local Intelligence," New York Times (Oct. 3, 1863), in ProQuest Historical Newspapers: The New York Times (1851-2009), p. 2; "News from Washngton: the Hospitalities to Russians," New York Times (Oct. 2, 1863), in ProQuest Historical Newspapers: The New York Times (1851-2009), p. 4; "The Russian Admiral to be Received at Boston," New York Times (Oct. 4, 1863), in ProQuest Historical Newspapers: The New York Times (1851-2009), p. 4.

90 Doris Kearns Goodwin, Team of Rivals: the Political Genius of Abraham Lincoln (New York: Simon & Schuster, paper 2006), pp. 546-547.

91 U.S. National Archives, College Park, Md., NA Identifier: 518056, Local Identifier: 59-DA-43. Department of State, Division of Historical Policy Research, Record Group 59: Photographs Relating to Diplomatic Affairs and International Relations, compiled 1783-1955. [Photograph created 08/1863, perhaps at Trenton Falls, N.Y.]

92 Marshall B. Davidson, "A Royal Welcome for the Russian Navy," American Heritage, Vol. 11, no. 4 (June 1960), p. 38.

93 Andrew J. Russell, Russell's Civil War Photographs: 116 Historic Prints (N.Y.: Dover, Publications, 1982); Tim O'Keeffe & Carl Peterson, Archivist, "Civil War Photos Provide History Lesson," The Colgate Scene (March 2004), online. Andrew J. Russell of Nunda, NY, took a photograph of Russian sailors aboard their warship prepared for a formal visit, probably in Alexandria, Virginia, in late 1863 or early 1864. The Russian Frigate Osliaba was photographed in the Harper's Weekly for October 3, 1863.

94 Doris Kearns Goodwin, op. cit., p. 593.

95 Marshall B. Davidson, op. cit., p. 38.

96 Douglas Kroll, "Friends in Peace and War": the Russian Navy's Landmark Visit to Civil War San Francisco (Washington, DC: Potomac, 2007), p. 126

97 "Russian Sailor killed in Annapolis," website. Jane Wilson McWilliams, Annapolis: City on the Severn (Baltimore, Md.: The Johns Hopkins University Press, 2011), pp. 182-183; Ed Okonowicz, Annapolis Ghosts: History, Mystery, Legends and Lore (Baltimore Md.: Victor Graphics, 2007), pp. 70-72.

98 Ibid.

99 Maryland, Journal of Proceedings of the House of Delegates: January Session [1864], (Annapolis, Md.: Bull & Tuttle, 1864), Feb. 5, 1864, pp. 242-243 and Feb. 10, 1864, p. 342.

100 Douglas Kroll, op. cit., pp. 78-81 and 162-163.

101 A. A. Woldman, op. cit., p. 164.

102 A. A. Woldman, op. cit., pp 191-193.

103 Hans L. Trefousse, Andrew Johnson: a Biography (N.Y.: W. W. Norton, 1989, paper 1991), pp. 189 and 212. A photo of the review of troops in late May of 1865 is found on p. 203.

104 A. A. Woldman, op. cit., p. 263. See also: U.S. Statutes at Large, 39th Congress (1865-67), p. 357. Abraham Lincoln was shot on April 14 and died on April 15, 1865, in Washington, D.C. Dmitri Karakozov attempted to assassinate Emperor Alexander II of Russia on April 4, 1866 in St. Petersburg. Hans L. Trefousse, Andrew Johnson: a Biography (NY: W. W. Norton, 1989, pbk., 1991), pp. 288 and 348. Albert A. Woldman, Lincoln and the Russians (World Pub. Co., 1952; reprint by Westport Conn.: Greenwood Press, 1970), pp. 277-289.

105 Jerry Harlowe, "Swan Song," Military Images, Southeastern, Vol. 21, issue 1 (July / Aug. 1999), p. 20-23, in ProQuest: Research Library. See also: A. A. Woldman, op. cit., pp. 263, 267-268.

106 "Operations of the Cruisers--Union," Official Record of the Union and Confederate Navies in the War of the Rebellion (Washington: 1896), Series I, Vol. 3, pp. 515 and 529.

107 A. A. Woldman, op.cit., pp. 277-290; Philip Shriver Klein, op. cit., pp. 325-326.

108 Hans Trefousse, Thaddeus Stevens: Nineteenth Century Egalitarian (Chapel Hill, NC: UNC Press, 1997), p. 214.

109 Our Documents: 100 Milestone Documents from the National Archives (Oxford, 2003), p. 103 [1868]; Dft. No. 9759 on Treasury Warrant No. 927, ARC Identifier 301667, U.S. National Archives, Washington, DC. In 1838, a wealthy English scientist names James Smithson had willed his estate to the US government to found "an establishment for the increase and diffusion of knowledge." The US would not accept paper bills of a check from the United

Kingdoms. "The bequest came across the Atlantic in a packet ship laden with half a million dollars' worth of gold coins, arriving in New York harbor on August 28, 1838." Daniel Walker Howe, <u>What Hath God Wrought: the Transformation of America, 1815-1848</u> (NY: Oxford, 2007, pbk. 2009), p. 468.

110 US National Archives, "Czar's Ratification of the Alaska Purchase Treaty," 06/20/1867, p. 1.

111 US National Archives, ARC Identifier 301666, Draft for Payment for the Purchase of Alaska, August 1, 1868.

112 <u>The Papers of Andrew Johnson</u>, Vol. 15 (September 1868-April 1869), ed. by Paul H. Bergeron (Knoxville: University of Tennessee Press, 1999), pp. 25-26.

113 <u>Boyd's Directory of Washington and Georgetown</u>, 1869 and 1871 (Washington: Boyd and Waite).

114 "Not Yet Arrived: the Grand Duke Not Here, Another Russian Frigate in the Bay," in New York <u>Times</u> (Nov. 17, 1871), ProQuest Historical Newspapers: The New York <u>Times</u> (1851-2009), p. 5.

115 <u>Boyd's Directory of the District of Columbia</u> (Washington: Boyd & Waite, 1872).

116 "Catacazy's Account of Himself—How the Russian Minister Blows His Own Horn," in New York <u>Times</u> (Nov. 17, 1871), op cit., p. 5.

117 Ben Perley Poore, <u>Pearley's Reminiscences of Sixty Years in the National Metropolis</u>, Vol. II (Philadelphia: Hubbard Brothers, 1886), pp. 276.

118 <u>The Papers of Ulysses S. Grant</u>, Vol. 22 (June 1, 1871-January 31, 1872), ed. by John Y. Simon (Carbondale and Edwardsville: Southern Illinois University Press, 1998), p. 130.

119 Ibid., p. 131n.

120 Ibid., pp. 148n-150n.

121 Ibid., p. 150n.

122 Ben Perley Poore, op cit, pp. 276-278.

123 Ibid., p. 276-277.

124 Suzanne Massie, "A Royal Visit: The Grand Duke Alexis in the United States,' in <u>The Tsar and the President: Alexander II and Abraham Lincoln, Liberator and Emancipator</u>, ed. by Marilyn Pfeifer Swezey (Washington: The American-Russian Cultural Cooperation Foundation, 2008), pp. 59-66. Douglas Kroll, <u>"Friends in Peace and War": the Russian Navy's Landmark Visit to Civil War San Francisco</u> (Washington: Potomac, 2007), p. 157.

125 Oliver Wendell Holmes, "Welcome to the Grand Duke Alexis," [Music Hall, December 9, 1871] and "At the Banquet to the Grand Duke Alesis" [December 9, 1871], in <u>Poetical Works</u> (Boston: Houghton Mifflin, 1887), pp. 255-257. Original from University of California, digitized by Internet

Archive. See also a photograph of the Grand Duke Alexis at the residente of the Hon. G. V. Fox, in Lowell, Massachusette, dated Dec. 9, 1871, in the Library of Congress Online Catalog, Prints and Photography, Stereograph Cards, Russia, #61.

126 The Papers of Ulysses S. Grant, Vol. 22, pp. 270-271.

127 Boyd's Directory of the District of Columbia, 1872, op cit, p. 584.

128 Boyd's Directory of the District of Columbia, 1873-75. See also: Энциклопедия российско-американских отношений, XVIII-XX века, ред. Е. А. Иванян (Москва: Мужданародные отношения, 2001), p. 676.

129 Boyd's Directory of the District of Columbia, 1876-1880.

130 "Ministers of Foreign Affairs (Russia)"—Wikipedia, the free encyclopedia. "Mysterious Muscovites: Shishkin in New York: New Arrivals: About Cruisers," in The Washington Post (1877-1954); May 10, 1878; ProQuest Historical Newspapers The Washington Post 1877-1992), p. 1.

131 Boyd's Directory of the District of Columbia, 1881-1882.

132 "The Struve family,"—Wikipedia, the free encyclopedia, Karl von Struve line (3rd gen).

133 Boyd's Directory of the District of Columbia, 1885-1892.

134 Marian (Hooper) Adams, The Letters of Mrs. Henry Adams, 1865-1883, ed. by Ward Thoron (Boston: Little, Brown, & Co., 1936), pp. 376-377.

135 "International Meridian Conference,"—Wikipedia, the free encyclopedia. Delegates for Russia included Mr. C. E. Struve, Envoy Extraordinary and Minister Plenipotentiary, Major-General Stebnitzki, Imperial Russian Staff, and Mr. J. de Kologrivoff, Conseiller d'Etat actuel.

136 Boyd's Directory of the District of Columbia, 1887-1890. "The Struve family,"—Wikipedia, the free encyclopedia, Karl von Struve line (3rd gen).

137 Semen Markovich Dubnov, History of the Jews in Russia and Poland, Vol. I (USA: KRAV Pub. House, 1975, reprint of 1916), pp. 378-393.

138 Ibid., p. 394.

139 Ibid., pp. 395-407.

140 Ibid., pp. 420-421.

141 Suzanne Massie, Land of the Firebird: the Beauty of Old Russia (N.Y.: Simon & Schuster, A Touchstone Book, 1980, rep. 1982), p. 415.

142 Elkhonon Yoffe, Tchaikovsky in America (N.Y.: Oxford University Press, 1986), p. 137.

143 Ibid., pp. 137-138.

144 Ibid., pp. 138-139. Quote from Tchaikovsky's diary.

145 Boyd's Directory of the District of Columbia, 1893-1894. "New Russian Minister," in The New York Times (August 6, 1892).

146 Alexander, Grand Duke of Russia, Once a Grand Duke (N.Y.: Farrar & Rinehart, 1932), pp. 120-127.

147 Ibid.

148 Ibid., pp. 241-243.

149 Boyd's Directory of the District of Columbia, 1895.

150 "Prince Cantacuzene Leaves Us: Russia's Representative Changes Places with Stuttgart Minister—Prince Cantaeuzene's Debut," in New York Times (Oct. 25, 1895).

151 Mexico Independent [NY] (Wednesday, May 20, 1896), col. a.

152 Lockport Daily Journal [NY] (Monday, Oct. 11, 1897), p. 2.

153 U.S. Department of State, Diplomacy in Action, (Foreign Embassies in the U.S. and Their Ambassadors, Office of the Chief of Protocol: report) (September 17, 2008), "April 1898 list—Legation Raised to Embassy– Listed as Embassy of Russia." Waldon Fawcett, "Envoys at Washington," The Cosmopolitan (May 1901), p. 381-386.

154 Boyd's Directory of the District of Columbia, 1899-1905. John C. G. Röhl, Wilhelm II: The Kaiser's Personal Monarchy, 1888-1900 (Cambridge, Eng: University Press, 2004), p. 205.

155 Charles M. Pepper, Every-day Life in Washington: with Pen and Camera (N.Y.; The Christian Herald, 1900), pp. 218-219.

156 Carol Felsenthal, Princess Alice: the Life and Times of Alice Roosevelt Longworth (St. Martin's Griffin, 2007), p. 65.

157 Chauncey M. Depew, "Ambassadors & Ministers," Chapter XVI of My Memories of Eighty Years (NY: C. Scribner's Sons, 1922), p. 197.

158 Stephen Bonsal, Suitors and Suppliants: the Little Nations at Versailles (N.Y.: Prentice Hall, 1946), p. 24.

159 Gregoire de Wollant [De-Vollan, Grigorii], The Land of the Rising Sun (N.Y.: Neale, 1905); see also Confederate Veteran, vol. 13, no. 1 (January 1905), p. 472.

160 Stephen Bonsal, op cit, p. 24.

161 Carol Felsenthal, op cit, p. 65.

162 Ibid.

163 http://www.imdb.com/name/nm0144312/bio; IMDb>Oleg Cassini>Biography. An Amazon.com Company.

164 "100 years ago--Russia's Jewish Question," in the International Herald Tribune (Monday, May 19, 2003).

165 "Russia Is Stirred," Tri-County Chronicle [Cass City, Michigan] (June 22, 1901), p. 1, col. 1.

166 Tom Isbell, Teddy Roosevelt and the Treasure of Ursa Major, in a special project with the White House Historical Association, the Kennedy Center staging an exciting new musical inspired by President Theodore Roosevelt and his family, Oct. 13-16, 2006, Family Theater, Kennedy Center, Washington, DC. Songs by Mark Russell; book was written by Ronald Kidd and Tom

Isbell (N.Y.: Simon and Schuster, 2008). Cassini was played by Richard Pelzman.

167 Boyd's District of Columbia Directory, 1906-1911.

168 Roman Rosen, from Wikipedia, the free encyclopedia.

169 Oak Hill Cemetery, Georgetown, DC, Lot 516 (East), Baron Roman Rosen, Russian Ambassador to the USA (Feb, 25, 1847-Dec. 31, 1921).

170 George Bakhmeteff, from Wikipedia, the free encyclopedia.

171 Boyd's District of Columbia Directory, 1912-1915.

172 "Mme. Bakhmeteff, Leader of Society Here, Dies in Paris," (Special Cable Dispatch), from The Washington Post (1923-1934); Jun. 27, 1925; ProQuest Historical Newspapers: The Washington Post (1877-1996), p. 2.

173 Ibid.

174 George Bakhmeteff, from Wikipedia, the free encyclopedia.

175 Boyd's District of Columbia Directory, 1916-1917.

176 Federal Writers' Project, Works Progress Administration, Washington: City and Capital (American Guide Series) (Washington: USGPO, 1937), p. 664.

177 Boris Bakhmeteff, from Wikipedia, the free encyclopedia.

178 Columbia University Libraries, Bakhmeteff Archive.

LILLARD, THE RUSSIANS ARE COMING . . ., SOURCES IN ORDER OF USE

Nicholas V. Riasanovsky, A History of Russia, 2n. ed. (NY: Oxford Univ. Press, 1969).

The United States and Russia: the Beginning of Relations, 1765-1815, ed. N. N. Bashkina, et al. (Joint Soviet-American Editorial Board, 1976-1979). English Language Edition.

Sally Somervell Mackall, Early Days in Washington (Washington: The Neale Co., 1899, Rep. 1934), pp. 114-123, and pp. 311-328.

Энциклопедия Российско-Американских Отношений, XVIII-XX, века. Ред. F. А. Ивапян (Москва: Международные Отношения, 2001).

Russkii Biograficheskii Slovar', (St. Petersburg, 1902).

Steven A. Usitalo and William Benton Whisenhurt, eds., Russia and Soviet History: from the time of troubles to the collapse of the Soviet Union. (Lanham, Mass.: Rowan & Littlefield, 2008), pp. 115-118.

George Washington Parke Custis, oration, *The Celebration of the Russian Victories, in Georgetown, District of Columbia, on the 5th of June, 1813*, (Georgetown, DC: J. B. Carter, 1813).

Rufus Rockwell Wilson, <u>Washington, the Capital City</u>, Vol. I (Philadelphia: J. B. Lippincott, 1902).

<u>Washington Directory</u>, comp. by Judah Delano. (Washington: William Duncan, 1822).

Website: Daniel L. Schlafly, Jr., High Beam Encyclopedia, 1997.

Petr Ivanovich Poletika, <u>A Sketch of the Internal Conditions of the United States of America, and of their political relations with Europe</u>. (Baltimore: E. J. Coale, 1826).

Daniel Walker Howe, "Monroe Doctrine," in <u>What Hath God Wrought: the transformation of America, 1815-1848</u>. (Oxford, 2007).

Suzanne Massie, <u>Land of the Firebird: the beauty of old Russia</u>. (N.Y.: Simon & Schuster, 1980).

<u>The Papers of Henry Clay</u>, eds. James F. Hopkins and Mary W. M. Hargreaves, Vol. 5 (1826). (University Press of Kentucky).

Joan M. Dixon, comp. <u>National Intelligencer, Newspaper Abstracts, 1824-1826</u>. (Bowis, MD, Heritage Books, 1999). P. 334.

James Monroe Museum and Memorial Library, Fredericksburg, Virginia. Jerod Kearney, Curator.

U.S. National Archives. Record Group 59. "Notes from the Russian Legation to the US Dept. of State, 1809-1906," Entry for April 20, 1826. College Park, Md.

William G. Allman and Melissa C. Naulin, <u>Something of Splendor: Decorative Arts from the White House: an exhibit</u>. (Washington: White House Historical Association, 2011).

"Washington in Jackson's Time . . .," ed. by Gaillard Hunt. Reprint in <u>Washington, D.C., a turn-of-the-century treasury</u>, ed. by F. Oppel and T. Meisel (1987).

E. S. Cohen & Co., <u>Full Directory, for Washington, Georgetown, and Alexandria: for 1834</u>. (Washington: Wm. Greer, 1834).

"Henry Walker Dead" (obituary), <u>The Washington Post</u> (Nov. 24, 1901), p. 2.

<u>Lippincott's Magazine of Popular Literature and Science</u> (Oct. 1873), Vol. 12, no. 31.

Alexis de Tocqueville, <u>Democracy in America</u>. 2 vols. (N.Y.: 1835).

Philip Shriver Klein. <u>President James Buchanan: a biography</u>. (University Park: Pennsylvania State University Press, 1962).

Allen Culling Clark, <u>Life and Letters of Dolly Madison</u>. (Washington: W. F. Roberts Co., 1914). [Mrs. Madison usually spelled her name, Dolley Madison.]

Richard F. Grimmett, <u>St. John's Church, Lafayette Square</u>. (Minneapolis: Mill City Press, 2009).

U.S. National Archives. Record Group 21, Probate in the District of Columbia, 1855, entry 115, [old series] o.s. 3500.

U.S. National Archives. Record Group 21, Probate in the District of Columbia, 1879, entry 115, [old series] o.s. 8340.

A. A. Woldman, <u>Lincoln and the Russians</u>. (N.Y.: 1952).

Harrison E. Salisbury, <u>War between Russian and China</u>. (N.Y.: W. W. Norton, 1969).

<u>The Tsar and the President: Alexander II and Abraham Lincoln, Liberator and Emancipator</u>, ed. by Marilyn Pfeifer Swezey. (Washington, DC: American-Russian Cultural Cooperation Foundation, 2008).

Susanne Sternthal, "The Curious Entente Cordial: President Lincoln and Tsar Alexander II," in <u>Russian Life</u> (July/August 2012), pp. 38-45.

Frank A. Golder, "Russian-American Relations during the Crimean War," in <u>The American Historical Review</u>, Vol. 31, No. 3 (April, 1926), pp. 462-476.

Douglas Kroll, <u>"Friends in Peace and War"</u>: <u>the Russian Navy's Landmark Visit to Civil War San Francisco</u>. (Washington: Potomac, 2007).

Doris Kearns Goodwin, <u>Team of Rivals: the Political Genius of Abraham Lincoln</u>. (N.Y.: Simon   & Schuster, 2005.

Marshall B. Davidson, "A Royal Welcome for the Russian Navy," in <u>American Heritage</u> (June 1960), Vol. 11, No. 4.

Ed Okonowicz, <u>Annapolis Ghosts: History, Mystery, Legends and Lore</u>. (Elkton, MD: Myst and Lace Publishers, 2007).

Hans L. Trefousse, <u>Andrew Johnson: a Biography</u>. (N.Y.: W.W. Norton, 1989).

<u>Official Records . . . Union and Confederate Navies</u>. (Washington, 1896), Series I, Vol. 3, pp. 515 and 529.

Jerry Harlow, "Swan Song," in <u>Military Images</u>, vol. 21, no. 1 (July/Aug. 1999), pp. 20-23.

<u>Colton's Map of the World</u>. (N.Y.: J. H. Colton & Co., 1855), with annotations by Mr. Collins' "Proposed Overland Pacific Telegraph, San Francisco to Moscow." Center for Legislative Archives, Record Group 233, Records of the U.S. House of Representatives, 1789-2006. ARC Identifier 306678. U.S. National Archives, Washington, DC.

<u>The Papers of Andrew Johnson</u>, Vol. 15 (Sept. 1868-April 1869), ed. by Paul H. Bergeron. (Knoxville, TN: University of Tennessee Press, 1999), pp. 25-26.

Donald R. Hickey, <u>The War of 1812: a Forgotten</u> Conflict. University of Illinois Press, 1989).

Benjamin Perley Poore, <u>Pearley's Reminiscences of Sixty Years in the National Metropolis</u>, Vol. II (Philadelphia: Hubbard Brothers, 1886), pp. 274-8.

The Papers of Ulysses S. Grant, Vol. 22 (June 1, 1871-January 31, 1872), ed. by John Y. Simon. (Carbondale and Edwardsville: Southern Illinois University Press, 1998).

<u>Harper's New Monthly Magazine</u> (June-Nov. 1863), p. 848.

<u>Harper's Weekly</u> (Oct. 17, 1863), pp. 661-5.

Mariam Hoooper Adams, <u>The Letters of Mrs Henry Adams, 1865-1883</u>, ed. by Ward Thoron (Boston: Little, Brown, 1936), pp. 376-7.

Semen Markovich Dubnov, <u>History of the Jews in Russia and Poland</u>, Vol. I (KTAV Pub., House, 1975, rep. of 1916). Chapter 28, pp. 378-427.

Charles M. Pepper, Every-day Life in Washington: with Pen aned Camera. (New York: Christian Herald, 1900), pp. 218-9.

Carol Felsenthal, Princess Alice: the Life and Times of Alice Roosevelt Longworth. (N.Y.: St. Martin's Griffin, 2007). "The President's Daughter," pp. 65+.

Boyd's District of Columbia Directory.

Chauncey M. Depew, Chapter XVI, "Ambassadors and Ministers," in My Memories of Eighty Years, (NY: Charles Scribner's Sons, 1922).

Gregorie de Wollant, The Land of the Rising Sun. (N.Y.: Neale, 1905).

Stephen Bonsal, Suitors and Suppliants: The Little Nations at Versailles. (N.Y.: Prentice Hall, 1946).

Tom Isbell, Teddy Roosevelt and the Treasure of Ursa Major, songs by Mark Russell. Performed in Washington, DC, at the Kennedy Center Family Theatre, during October 2006. Cassini was played by Richard Pelzman. Book was written by Ronald Kidd and Tom Isbell (N.Y.: Simon and Schuster, 2008).

Federal Writers' Project. Washington: City and Capital. (American Guide Series) Washington: GPO, 1937.

Maryland. Journal of Proceedings of the House of Delegates. January 1864 Session. Pp. 242 [Feb. 5, 1864] and 342 [Feb. 10, 1864]. (Annapolis: Bull & Tuttle, 1864).

Oliver Wendell Holmes, "Songs of Welcome and Farewell," in Poetical Works. (Boston: Houghton Mifflin, 1887), pp. 255-7.

"Mme. Bakhmeteff . . . Dies in Paris," in the Washington Post (June 27, 1925), p. 2.

Elkonon Yoffe, <u>Tchaikovsky in America</u>. (N.Y.: Oxford University Press, 1986).

Alexander, Grand Duke of Russia, <u>Once a Grand Duke</u>. (N.Y.: Farrar & Rinehart, 1932).